GOSPEL
DIALOGUE

Gospel Dialogue

WATCHMAN NEE

Christian Fellowship Publishers, Inc.
New York

Available from the Publishers at:
Box 1021
Manassas, Virginia 22110

Printed in the United States of America

CONTENTS

Contents

Contents

This volume contains the gist of a dialogue on the truth of the gospel that was held between the author and other Christian believers in Shanghai, China, during the period of 1930–1931.

Scripture quotations are from the American Standard Version of the Bible (1901), unless otherwise indicated.

GOSPEL DIALOGUE

Question 1

Since the Bible declares that "by grace have ye been saved" (Eph. 2.8), then we need to ask the following questions:

Is grace (a) given to whoever is *deserving,* that is, does God require man to do good in order to be saved?

(b) given to *supplement* what is lacking, that is, does God require man to do his best before he is saved?

(c) *withheld* because of the lack of merit, that is, can God refuse to save a person because he is no good?

(d) given *less* to the less deserving, that is, can God refuse to save a man because he is not as good as another man?

Does grace (e) make the recipient a *debtor,* that is to say, is the word "recompense" proper to use here?

(f) absolve *directly* the sinner's sin, that is, can God freely forgive a person out of compassion for the sinner?

(g) absolve *directly* the believer's sin, that is, can God freely forgive a person out of love for the believer?

Answer:

We human beings possess the greatest of defects, which is, that we tend to measure God's heart by our own. Our human heart is one of law, not one of grace. We always imagine God as having a heart like ours, hence we often misunderstand Him.

We must be clear as to what grace is: (a) Grace is not given to whoever is deserving. "Now to him that worketh, the reward is not reckoned as of grace, but as of debt" (Rom. 4.4). Stated conversely, though, to him who does *not* deserve and yet to whom is given, *that* is grace. If it is deserved, it cancels the very idea of grace. Grace is what it is because there is not the tiniest element of merit in it. "For by grace have ye been saved" (Eph. 2.8). To save the *un*deserved is grace. "Being justified freely by his [God's] grace" (Rom. 3.24). What is meant by "freely"? In the original Greek, "freely" is the same word as is translated "without a cause" in John 15.25 where the Lord is recorded as saying, "They hated me without a cause", quoting from the Old Testament. To say that the grace of God justifies freely simply means that God justifies us without any cause or reason. "The scripture shut up all things under sin" and "God hath shut up all unto disobedience" (Gal. 3.22; Rom. 11.32). God has placed all men on the same footing so that none may be saved by works (that is, by doing good), but that all must be saved by grace. Were you to ask Paul how he was saved, he would surely answer that he was saved by the grace of God. Were you to ask all the saints the same question, they would all give the same answer: saved by grace. God saves us without a cause; and this is grace.

(b) Grace is not given to supplement what is lacking in man. "Not of works, that no man should glory" (Eph. 2.9). This does not mean that there need be no good works after being saved; it simply indicates that man is not saved by works. If man were saved by works he would surely have something of which to boast. Were he saved with just ten percent of works, man would have ten percent of boasting but God would lose ten percent of glory. Yet God will not share His glory with man. He hates man's self-bragging, for His purpose is for Him himself to be glorified. Hence the grace of God is not supplementary to what is lacking in man.

Grace is neither given to him who is deserving nor given as a bonus to the deserved. It is neither a fair reward nor an overabundant recompense. The question of "deservingness" or one's worthiness has absolutely no common ground with grace. To receive grace is to cast aside completely this matter of worthiness. The thought of anyone's being more or less worthy to be saved is entirely unfounded. Concerning salvation, none is able to obtain the grace of God by any works of his own.

People often think if they try their best to do good and to keep the law, that they can then depend on the grace of God for what they cannot do. This is plainly a depending on works for a certain percentage and on grace for a certain percentage. On one occasion a man was heard to declare: "We must keep the Ten Commandments, or else we cannot be saved." "Have you ever violated the commandments?" he was asked. "Indeed, I have." "What, then, do you do?" "What I cannot do, I rely on the grace of God for," said he. Such thinking shows an ignorance of grace.

That young man in Matthew 19 asked the Lord Jesus: "What good thing shall I do, that I may have eternal life?" And the Lord said to him: "Keep the commandments." Having heard that this young man had observed all these things, the Lord then said: "If thou wouldst be perfect, go, sell that which thou hast, and give to the poor." In hearing this the young man went away sorrowful, because he could not do it (vv.16–22). Truly, if a person desires to be saved by keeping the law he must do it "all". He not only must love God with all his heart, all his soul, all his mind, and all his strength, but must also give away all he possesses without exception. But if he depends on the grace of God, he should rely on it wholly. It is never done partly by man and partly by God, for the grace of God is not to supplement the inadequacy of man. It is a case of either purely the grace of God or entirely the works of man. It cannot be partly of man and partly of God.

Why is this so? Because the Lord Jesus has already died. As God has put all sinners on the same footing, therefore, when the Lord Jesus was crucified, God "laid on him the iniquity of us all" (Is. 53.6). The problem of sin is thus solved once and for all. For this reason, man cannot trust in his own merit before God; otherwise the work of Christ would be overturned as though He had died in vain.

(c) Grace is not withheld because of the lack of merit. (This is quite similar to the first point of this question; only here, the matter is approached negatively.) On the contrary, grace is given *because* of man's unworthiness. It is only at the time when man knows his utter helplessness that he will cry out for grace. It is also at this juncture that God will dispense grace. If a man himself has the strength he will not think of asking for grace, and so God need not give grace. Consequently, the lack of merit will not in any way hinder God from giving grace; quite the opposite, it is the sole condition for God to grant His grace.

"Grace is boundless mercy shown in boundless goodness," one brother has said. What is grace? Grace is that which flows from the top to the bottom. What is love? Love is a treating as equal. What is respect? Respect is that which is shown to those who are over you. But grace flows downward. Grace has only this one direction. In order to obtain the grace of God, you must acknowledge yourself as a helpless sinner—this alone gives you the qualification for receiving God's grace.

Many dislike grace because it requires a humbling act on their part. Grace compels you to concur that you are the worst person. For just as no inverted cup can receive water, so no proud person is able or willing to accept the salvation of God. We need to admit our uselessness before we can receive the grace of God.

(d) Grace is not given less to the less deserving. (This is the opposite to what the second point of this question speaks about.) God does not overlook the problem of man's sin. As a matter of fact, He is most strict, definite, and thorough in His dealing with man's sin. Through His Son He has dealt most completely with this problem. Hence how can there be raised the question of deserving or not deserving, the matter of being more worthy or less worthy? The grace of God never questions man's "undeservingness". Before God, all men are the same, and all may have His grace.

Since God will not withhold grace because of man's unworthiness (rather, He gives grace for that very reason), how can He ever make any distinction among the unworthy ones as to who are the less unworthy and who are the least unworthy in His dispensing of grace?

God will not give less grace to those who sin more and more grace to those who sin less. For grace is not used by God to mend the holes of sinners. In the realm of grace, both the sinner himself and his works are completely set aside.

Since grace is gratuitous, it is not at all conditional on the state of the recipient. He on his part does not earn grace for any reason whatsoever. Grace is not withheld because of the lack of merit. It has absolutely no relationship to the condition of the recipient. It will not be given in less measure to the comparatively more unworthy. Otherwise, grace would be conditional on the state of the recipient. Hence grace is given neither according to the man himself nor according to his relative position with other people. God's grace is so vast and measureless that it is intended for all kinds of sinners. Those who consider themselves as fairly good need the grace of God as much as those who are looked upon as the chief of sinners.

People may perhaps speculate that the better ones certainly deserve a little more. But according to God, all are the same. For example, several bowls fall to the ground and are broken. Some may break into two pieces; some, five pieces; and some, into powder. Although their broken condition varies, they are all broken nonetheless. Whether you are "a little better" sinner or you are "the worst" of sinners, you are nevertheless a sinner. The Bible declares that all have sinned. In sending the Lord Jesus to the world to die for sinners, God gives opportunity to all sinners to be saved. Even if there is but a single man in the entire world who needs to be saved, God is still willing to send His Son to die for him. Does not the parable of the shepherd seeking the one lost sheep tell us that he leaves the ninety-nine and goes after the one lost sheep? (Luke 15.3,4) As long as you are a lost sheep, and regardless of your being a great or a small sinner, you need the Lord Jesus to die for you.

(e) Grace does not make the recipient a debtor. When someone advances a certain amount of money to you and lets you enjoy it temporarily but requires you to repay the same amount afterwards—that is called a debt. Wages are dispensed according to your works. Grace is neither given as wages according to your works nor lent temporarily as debt to be repaid afterward. God saves us by grace; our salvation is not something God lends out to us. If it is lent, it must be repaid by us later on; but then it cannot be considered as grace. Grace does not mean that, seeing our current lack of merit in works, God lends us salvation at first but requires us to keep our salvation by adding on to it our merit afterward. For grace charges nothing—past, present, and future. Should God give us something now but require us to repay in the future, it is then a debt and not grace. But the grace of God is given freely to all the undeserved, without charging anything at any time.

People conceive an incorrect idea: yes, we are saved by grace, but we must thereafter keep this salvation by our own selves. This is an error. The Bible never tells us that God's grace has made us debtors. "The free gift of God is eternal life in Christ Jesus our Lord" (Rom. 6.23). What is the nature of this eternal life? It is a gift. In other words, it is something which God bestows as a gift. Must it be repaid? Let us be clear that, it not being a debt, grace needs no repayment—neither now nor many days later. This is not meant to imply, of course, that a Christian does not need to have good works or to serve God with faithfulness. After one is saved, he should perform good works and ought to serve

God faithfully. Yet the motive behind such actions is the love of Christ, and the power for doing these things is the Holy Spirit. Good works and faithful service we must have, but they are not for the sake of earning salvation nor for the sake of keeping salvation. The works of a Christian are not used to pay back the debt of salvation which God has given. Just as God saves us out of His love for us, even so must we serve God out of our love for Him. Just as God does not give salvation as a loan, so we do not serve God faithfully as a form of repayment.

How many there are who do not understand the grace of God clearly! They assume that before one is saved, and though he is unworthy, God is still willing to save him; but that after he is saved he has to do good, or else God will withdraw His salvation. This is like a purchase which is made on the installment plan. The merchandise is first delivered and subsequently payments are made by installment; failure to pay on time will result in confiscation of the merchandise by the seller. Such a concept plainly distorts the grace of God. When we are saved God gives us eternal life; yet He never asks us to pay back by installments, nor will He take His salvation back even if we perform no good deeds afterward.

Moreover, since eternal life is a gift, how can anyone speak of repaying? Such a word is certainly wrong. We serve God out of love. For instance, suppose my father gives me a gift and yet I say I will repay him. I save for months and years to accumulate enough money to pay him back. By so doing, however, does it not turn out that I am in reality buying that gift? Grace never charges anything, else it would not be grace at all.

(f) Grace does not directly absolve a sinner's sin. This matter is frequently misunderstood by many believers.

They reckon that God forgives the sins of a sinner out of His liberality. Not at all. In forgiving a sinner God is not compromising, nor does He pretend either to be deaf or to overlook anything. This the Bible clearly never says. "As sin reigned in death, even so might grace reign through righteousness unto eternal life through Jesus Christ our Lord" (Rom. 5.21). Sin reigns by itself, but grace reigns through righteousness. Grace does not reign by its own self. Let it be known that God not only has grace but He also has righteousness. He delights in having men saved, but He also delights in protecting their salvation with righteousness. He gives grace to us not because of His carelessness, but because of His having solved the problem of our sin.

If we mistake God's grace as His liberality, then the cross of Christ is both unnecessary and meaningless. True, there can be no cross of Christ without the love of God. Yet God's love alone, in the absence of His righteousness, will never demand the cross of Christ. God is very much aware of our sins; He cannot overlook them. And since we have no way of solving the problem of our sins, God causes His Son to bear them in His body upon the cross in order to have the problem of sin solved forever. This is the grace of God. God's grace solves the problem of sin first before it absolves sin. The Lord must die as our substitute that we may be saved.

A sinner is reckoned as such because (1) his conduct is bad; (2) his nature is corrupted; and (3) God's righteous law has so judged. In saving a sinner, God must (1) forgive the sins of his bad conduct; (2) regenerate him by giving him a new life; and (3) justify him. Now the Lord Jesus has already suffered the penalty of sin and died for us; therefore God cannot but forgive us. It is an erroneous concept among some people that we need to turn the heart of God by much begging. Not so. We are forgiven because God's righteous wrath over our sin has already been discharged upon the Lord Jesus. We may therefore praise and thank God, saying, that since the Lord Jesus has already been judged and that righteousness can demand penalty only once, we shall not be penalized anymore.

(g) Grace does not absolve directly a believer's sin. The principle involved here is the same as the foregoing one. After a person is saved, if he is incidentally overcome by sin and later repents of his sin, he does not obtain forgiveness through constant begging. It is not by asking God to make provision for forgiveness today; rather, it is by believing in what Christ has already done on the cross. God is righteous; He cannot but forgive those who have accepted salvation since the Lord Jesus has already died. So, if a Christian should inadvertently sin, he needs to be clear on the following four points: (1) that he receives forgiveness by confessing his own sin (1 John 1.9); (2) that forgiveness is available for all sin (1 John 1.7,9—noting especially "cleanseth us from *all* sin" and "cleanse us from *all* unrighteousness"); (3) that before he prays, God is already willing to forgive, because the Lord Jesus acts as the believer's Advocate with the Father (1 John 2.1,2); and (4) that God thus forgives and cleanses because of His faithfulness and righteousness on the one hand and because of Jesus Christ the Righteous on the other.

Question 2

Is there any difference between "transgression" and "iniquity" in the Bible?

Answer:

"Transgression" and "iniquity" are two Old Testament terms. These two words reveal the two aspects of the Old Testament concept of sin. Transgression is subjective, while iniquity is objective. Transgression points to our conduct, whereas iniquity points to our condition before God. In the world we have committed transgression, before God we have committed iniquity. "I said, I will confess my transgressions unto Jehovah; and thou forgavest the iniquity of my sin" (Ps. 32.5). "I will cleanse them from all their iniquity, whereby they have sinned against me; and I will pardon all their iniquities, whereby they have sinned against me" (Jer. 33.8). From this we can readily see that iniquity is the condition of man before God after he has sinned or transgressed. When man sins, violates God's law, and offends God, in God's sight he has committed iniquity. In the books of Exodus and Leviticus it is frequently mentioned how the priests who serve in the sanctuary must bear their iniquity under certain situations. The Hebrew word used is *avon,* translated as iniquity, not the word *pesha,* translated as transgression (see Ex. 28.38,43; Lev. 5.1,17). Iniquity is a thing before God, that which is borne and redeemed in the sanctuary. For this reason, when the verse in Daniel 9.24 speaks of "transgression" and "sins", it says "finish" and "make an end of"; but when the same verse speaks of "iniquity", it says "make reconciliation for" (ASV) or "make expiation for" (Darby), thus showing that the latter is a matter before God. We also see that the destruction of Sodom is due to the iniquity of the city (Gen. 19.15; also cf. 15.16).

Whenever "transgression" is mentioned in the Old Testament, it is always connected with action and conduct. Note, for example, the following: "He showeth them their work, and their transgressions, that they have behaved themselves proudly" (Job 36.9); "In the transgression of the lips is a snare to the evil man" (Prov. 12.13); "Whoso robbeth his father or his mother, and saith, It is no transgression, the same is the companion of a destroyer" (Prov. 28.24); "The transgression of Jacob is all this, and for the sins of the house of Israel. What is the transgression of Jacob? is it not Samaria? and what are the high places of Judah? are they not Jerusalem?" (Micah 1.5) Things such as pride, stealing, and idolatry are all viewed as transgressions.

Note also these verses. "I will judge you, O house of Israel, every one according to his ways, saith the Lord Jehovah. Return ye, and turn yourselves from all your transgressions; so iniquity shall not be your ruin. Cast away from you all your transgressions, wherein ye have transgressed; and make you a new heart and a new spirit: for why will ye die, O house of Israel?" (Ez. 18.30,31); "Thus saith Jehovah: For three transgressions of Damascus, yea, for four, I will not turn away the punishment thereof" (Amos 1.3). Transgression is so serious because it may produce iniquity. But thank God, all the problems of our transgression and iniquity have already been solved through the redemptive work of Christ: "He was wounded for our transgressions, he was bruised for our iniquities" (Is. 53.5).

Question 3

Is there any difference between the "blessed" in Romans 4.7 and the "blessed" in Romans 4.8? If there is, what is it?

Answer:

There is a difference, it being the difference between forgiveness of sin and justification. The blessed in verse 7 is negative, while the blessed in verse 8 is positive. Verse 7 speaks of how God forgives iniquities and covers sins; verse 8 speaks of how He so works in a man as to make the latter appear as one who has never sinned—"not reckon sin" means being justified.

What is the difference between forgiveness and justification? Forgiveness is saying that you have sinned but God forgives your sin. Justification is saying that you are a righteous man and you have never sinned. For instance, a person who is judged and condemned by the court to be punished with imprisonment is released by the same court at the time of amnesty—so that such legal action toward the man can be likened to his having received forgiveness. But if he is proclaimed as guiltless after being judged by the court, this to him is justification.

In saving us, the Lord not only forgives us but also justifies us. This is grace! Since the Lord solves the problem of our sins so completely by shedding His blood and since we are raised with Him in His resurrection, God looks upon us as though we had never sinned. God has made us as perfect as Christ by virtue of what He has already done in Christ. "Ye are complete in him [Christ]" (Col. 2.10 Darby). Now just as God looks on Christ and loves Christ, so He also looks on us and loves us. He sees us as being already complete in Christ.

Question 4

Are our sins "covered" (Rom. 4.7) or "put away" (Heb. 9.26)? Where is the distinction?

Answer:

Our sins are "put away", not "covered". For the word of Hebrews 9.26 clearly states that "once at the end of the ages hath he been manifested to *put away* sin by the sacrifice of himself".

Why does Romans 4.7 say "covered"? We should know that this is quoted from Psalm 32.1. Aside from this one place where the word in Psalms is quoted, nowhere else in the entire New Testament can a Scripture verse be found which states that our sins are covered before God. Hence the "covered" here must have reference to the sins of the people in the Old Testament time being covered. As a matter of fact, every sin committed during the Old Testament period was only covered until it was put away at the death of the Lord Jesus. For note this New Testament verse: "He is the mediator of a new covenant . . . for the redemption of the transgressions that were under the first covenant" (Heb. 9.15).

Let us be reminded, first of all, that the Hebrew word for "atonement" (*kaphar*) in the Old Testament means "to cover". Except in Romans 4.7 (which quotes the Old Testament), the New Testament never again uses this word. And secondly, the word "atonement" is connected mostly with sin-offering, that is, a sacrifice offered for the sake of sin. Jesus Christ is our propitiation, because He has offered himself for our sin. He does not merely cover our sin.

Let us recognize that the Lord Jesus comes to take away

our sin, and not just to cover it. "Behold, the lamb of God, that taketh away the sin of the world" (John 1.29).

Question 5

How often must sins be purified—once or many times?

Answer:

The purification of sins is made only once. "When [Christ] had made purification of sins, [He] sat down on the right hand of the Majesty on high" (Heb. 1.3). This indicates that His work of purification has already been done. "This he did once for all, when he offered up himself" (7.27). "Through his own blood, [Christ] entered in once for all into the holy place, having obtained eternal redemption" (9.12). "Nor yet that he should offer himself often, . . . but now once at the end of the ages hath he been manifested to put away sin by the sacrifice of himself" (9.25,26). "By which will we have been sanctified through the offering of the body of Jesus Christ once for all. . . . But he, when he had offered one sacrifice for sins for ever, sat down on the right hand of God" (10.10–12). All these passages show that sins are once purified.

The preciousness of the blood of Christ lies in its efficacy. Once it is shed, it purifies sins forever. Not so with the blood of bulls and goats, that "can never" by "the same sacrifices year by year" which are offered "continually, make perfect them that draw nigh. . . . Because the worshippers, having been once cleansed, would have had no more consciousness of sins. But in those sacrifices there is a remembrance made of sins year by year. For it is impossible that the blood of bulls and goats should take away sins" (Heb. 10.1–4). Does not this passage plainly tell us that the blood of bulls and goats only reminds people yearly of their sins, and that therefore the sacrifice must be offered continually? For the blood of bulls and goats cannot take away sins. Only the work of the cross is done once for all; and nothing more can be added.

How, then, are we to explain the word in 1 John 1.7—"If we walk in the light, as he is in the light, we have fellowship one with another, and the blood of Jesus his Son cleanseth us from all sin"? The cleansing here contains the thought of continual cleansing. Continuance is different from repetition. Repetition is to do something again and again, while continuance is a doing something without interruption. The blood of the Lord has permanent value before God, and it is continuously effective. It does not cleanse intermittently. The precious blood gives us the utmost liberty before God. We will not see the difference between the Lord's blood and the blood of bulls if we do not know how mightily effective is the blood of the Lord Jesus before God. A believer regains peace after he has sinned, not because the blood cleanses him once more but because, as he confesses his sin, he believes that the blood has cleansed him.

For instance, a sinner needs to be saved. Is he saved by believing that Christ has already died for him or by asking Christ to come and die once again for him today? We know without any doubt that a sinner is saved by simply believing on Christ who has died for him. Similarly, we need to ask this: Will a believer gain peace by believing in the blood of Christ that has cleansed his sin or by asking Christ to come and shed His blood once again so as to cleanse his sin?

Naturally he obtains peace by believing in the blood of Christ that has cleansed his sin.

Let us consider the type in Numbers 19 concerning the ashes of the red heifer. The red heifer to be offered as a sacrifice must fulfill three qualifications: (1) it must be without spot, having no blemish—typifying the sinlessness of the Lord himself; (2) it must never have been under any yoke—signifying how the Lord himself has never been a slave to Satan; and (3) it must be red in color (v.2)—representing how the Lord has borne our sins, for is it not written, "Though your sins be as scarlet" (Is. 1.18a)? The redness is in the hide and hair, not in the inside of the heifer, even as the Lord Jesus is sinless within himself and so merely bears the sin of many on the outside. The red heifer is burned without the camp (vv.3,5), but so does our Lord suffer "without the gate" (Heb. 13.12). The red heifer is used to atone for sin, because her blood is sprinkled toward the front of the tent of meeting (v.4) as is done in all the sacrifices for sin. If it were for purification, it would be sprinkled upon the man.

The *burning* of the red heifer is also different from the burning of other sacrifices. "And one shall burn the heifer in his sight; her skin, and her flesh, and her blood, with her dung, shall he burn: and the priest shall take cedar wood, and hyssop, and scarlet, and cast it into the midst of the burning of the heifer" (vv.5,6). Speaking representatively, cedarwood and hyssop include the whole creation ("from the cedar . . . even unto the hyssop" (1 Kings 4.33). The scarlet represents sin. And thus we know that at the death of the Lord Jesus the sin of the whole world from Adam onward was included in it. What the Lord has borne on the cross for our sin is absolute, unlimited, and without addition.

The red heifer is dead, but her ashes remain. Now her very ashes prove that a red heifer has been slain. Yet what is the use of the ashes? "For the unclean they shall take of the ashes of the burning of the sin-offering; and running water shall be put thereto in a vessel: . . . and the clean person shall sprinkle upon the unclean . . . and on the seventh day he shall purify him" (vv.17–19). The ashes have the continual efficacy of putting away sin. This indicates that as we once have trusted in the fact of the Lord's substitutionary death and have our sins forgiven, so shall all our sins be continually dealt with by this fact of the Lord's death for our forgiveness. The cleansing in 1 John 1.9–2.1 speaks of the same efficacy as that of the ashes of the red heifer.

Let us be well aware that if we inadvertently sin we do not have *another* red heifer to die for us; no, we have the same Red Heifer that has already died and whose ashes continue to be effectual before God. How we thank God for the fact that Christ has borne all our sins on the cross—this not only pays for our past debts but also leaves enough efficacy left to pay for our future debts. This is the Lord's doing! And this is the gospel!

Question 6

Why is the blood of the sin-offering in Leviticus 4.1–7 brought to the tent of meeting and sprinkled seven times before God before the veil of the sanctuary, whereas according to the law of the leper in the day of his cleansing the blood is sprinkled upon the leper seven times?

Answer:

The first thing for us to notice about this matter is this: in the entire Bible, who makes a demand for blood? It is God himself. Why does He require the blood? Why did He not forgive the sin of the children of Israel out of mercy? Had He done that, however, He would have been un- righteous. But, you may say, was it not enough for that publican mentioned in Luke 18 to cry for mercy? No, because what he actually asked of God was this: "God, be thou propitiated to me the sinner" (v.13 mg.). Sin must be judged and punished. God can forgive only when one comes to Him with the blood, for "apart from shedding of blood there is no remission" (Heb. 9.22). This is God's righteous- ness.

Some people may pray in this manner: "O God, if it pleases You to forgive, please forgive; if it is Your will to forgive, then forgive." We know, however, that forgiveness is not a question of God's like or dislike, nor is it a matter of His will. Although God is merciful and gracious and pleased to forgive, He nonetheless cannot forgive without the blood. The blood is absolutely necessary for God's forgiveness. For He is a righteous God.

To sprinkle the blood seven times before God is to satisfy or propitiate the righteous demand of God, and thus He is able to forgive man's sin. Where there is sin, there is the need for blood. This is the righteous demand of God. Let us illustrate it this way: Suppose a person commits the crime of murder and pleads for mercy at the court; and he is then forgiven by the judge out of mercy. Later on, the second and the third person will commit the same crime, plead for the same mercy, and receive the same forgiveness. Even if this would happen only three times in succession, the country would be thrown into chaos. For people will not be afraid to murder as long as they know they will be forgiven simply by asking for mercy. If sin goes unpunished, it would be considered unrighteous.

God's law demands death or a shedding of blood with respect to those who sin. The Lord Jesus has shed His precious blood to propitiate the demand of God's law. Therefore, we are saved not only because God has grace but also because He has righteousness. The blood of the sin-offering must be brought before God. Without the blood God cannot forgive man's sin even though He has the heart to forgive. For His righteousness does not allow Him to forgive a sinner without the "blood".

But what does it mean to sprinkle the blood seven times on the leper? Let us take note that what Leviticus 14.1–7 speaks of is not a being healed through the sprinkling of the blood; rather, it is speaking of a sprinkling that occurs *after* the leper is healed. Why, then, is the blood to be sprinkled at all? This is to tell us that even though the leper is healed, he is only cleansed before man. To be cleansed before God there needs to be the blood applied. God's demand is the blood. After the leper is healed he will be acceptable to man; but he remains unclean before God until there is blood sprinkled on him.

In Matthew 8.1–4 we find that after the Lord Jesus healed a leper He charged him to offer the gift that Moses demanded (for at that moment the Lord had not yet been crucified, and therefore He charged the leper to act in accordance with the ordinance of the Old Testament). Though the Lord had helped him to be cleansed before man, for him to be cleansed before God the leper still had a need for the blood. This shows us that no matter how good and moral a person may be, he is not cleansed in God's sight without the blood.

The blood is to satisfy God's demand. The blood is shed

not just to cleanse our conscience but also to fulfill God's lawful demand. We are sinners; without the blood we cannot be saved. We are saved not because we are worthy, but because the Lord has shed His blood. We are accepted by God only because there is the blood. We dare to approach God not on our own merit but on the merit of the shed blood of the Lord Jesus. The blood alone gives God satisfaction and grants us cleansing before Him.

Question 7

How are "sin" and "sins" differently used?

Answer:

The difference between sin and sins is that between sin stated in the singular number and sin stated in the plural number. In the Old Testament there is no distinction made of sin in singular and plural numbers. Only the New Testament expresses this difference, and it is a very significant difference too.

Let us list all the places in the New Testament where sin (Gk. *hamartia*) both in the singular and in the plural is used.

"Sin" in singular number: Matt.12.31; John 1.29; 8.34 (twice), 46; 9.41 (twice); 15.22 (twice), 24; 16.8,9; 19.11; Acts 7.60; Rom. 3.9,20; 4.8; 5.12 (twice), 13 (twice), 20,21; 6.1,2,6 (twice), 7,10,11,12,13,14,16,17,18,20,22,23; 7.7 (twice), 8 (twice), 9,11,13 (thrice), 14,17,20,23,25; 8.2,3 (mg., thrice), 10; 14.23; 1 Cor. 15.56 (twice); 2 Cor. 5.21

(twice); 11.7; Gal. 2.17; 3.22; 2 Thess. 2.3; Heb. 3.13; 4.15; 9.26,28 (the second "sin"); 10.6,8,18; 11.25; 12.1,4; 13.11; James 1.15 (twice); 2.9; 4.17; 1 Peter 2.22; 4.1; 2 Peter 2.14; 1 John 1.7,8; 3.4 (twice), 5 (the second "sin"), 8,9; 5.16 (twice), 17 (twice).

"Sins" in plural number: Matt. 1.21; 3.6; 9.2,5,6; 26.28; Mark 1.4,5; 2.5,7,9,10; Luke 1.77; 3.3; 5.20,21,23,24; 7.47,48,49; 11.4; 24.47; John 8.21, 24 (twice); 9.34; 20.23; Acts 2.38; 3.19; 5.31; 10.43; 13.38; 22.16; 26.18; Rom. 4.7; 7.5; 11.27; 1 Cor. 15.3,17; Gal. 1.4; Eph. 2.1; Col. 1.14; 1 Thess. 2.16; 1 Tim. 5.22,24; 2 Tim. 3.6; Heb. 1.3; 2.17; 5.1,3; 7.27; 8.12; 9.28 (the first "sins"); 10.2,3,4,11,12,17,26; James 5.15,20; 1 Peter 2.24 (twice); 3.18; 4.8; 2 Peter 1.9; 1 John 1.9 (twice); 2.2,12; 3.5 (the first "sins"); 4.10; Rev. 1.5; 18.4,5.

After we have read these many Scripture verses we may detect how wise is God in writing the Bible. We will truly say to Him: "O God, we worship You!"

The distinctive uses of "sin" and "sins" are as follows. Whenever the Bible refers to man's outward sinful conduct such as pride, jealousy, lying, and so forth, "sin" in the plural number is always used. "Sin" in the singular number is never used in the Bible for outward sin; instead, it is employed in two different ways: (1) *It points to the sin that reigns within or its power and dominion.* This is also commonly known by the terms: the root of sin or the denominator of sin. Actually these terms are not scripturally accurate; they are merely borrowed for the sake of convenience. The Bible never uses either of them, it instead speaks of sin as reigning like a king or having dominion like a master. "Sin" in the singular number is usually employed to specify the power which reigns over us and drives us to commit sins.

(2) *As a collective term, it sometimes refers to the whole problem of sin* (such as is found in John 1.29 and 1 John 1.7 which we discuss later). Whenever the Bible speaks of God forgiving sin it always uses the plural number "sins", because what we need to be forgiven of are the sins we commit in outward behavior. As regards the sinful nature within us, it cannot be solved by forgiveness. It would be a mistake to say God forgives "sin" and use the singular number. For God only forgives "sins". Since "sin" in the singular number is a master, a power, it is something we are not directly responsible for and is not to be settled through forgiveness. But "sins" in the plural number need forgiveness because these are our conduct for which we *are* held responsible, and they will cause a penalty to be levied against us if not forgiven. For this cause, whenever the Bible mentions the matter of confessing our sins, it should always be expressed as "confess our sins" (1 John 1.9), using the plural and not the singular number. "Sin" does not refer to man's conduct, and therefore does not require confession; but the term "sins" does signify man's conduct, requiring confession to be made. Christ's death is to save us from "sins" in the plural number. "Thou shalt call his name Jesus; for it is he that shall save his people from their sins" (Matt. 1.21). This means that the Lord Jesus saves us from all the sins in our conduct.

The Lord Jesus declared to the Jews: "Ye shall die in your sins" (John 8.24). Once again, this refers to sin in the plural number, and not to sin singular. Never once does the Bible say that Christ has died for our sin as expressed in the singular number; it always says that Christ has died for our sins plural.

"Ye were dead through your trespasses and sins" (Eph. 2.1). Note that the word "sin" here is in the plural form and not in the singular. It means that we spend our lives in sins such as pride, uncleanness, jealousy, and so forth. We were dead in plural "sins", not in "sin" in its singular number. Two more examples are these: (1) "should take away sins" in Hebrews 10.4 is a taking away of sins in the plural number; (2) "had no more consciousness of sins" in 10.2 is also an expression of sin in the plural.

Why do we have no more consciousness of sins after the blood of the Lord has cleansed our conscience? Because the sin which our conscience accuses us of before God is sin in the plural number; that is, one sin after another, such as ill-temper, pride, and so forth. Since the blood of the Lord Jesus has already obtained forgiveness for these our sins, naturally our conscience will no longer be conscious of them. Sins there most certainly are, but the blood has dealt with them. Had the blood of the Lord cleansed sin in its singular sense, no one would have been able to experience personally such a cleansing; because in cleansing sin in the singular number, it would have meant that we would never have again been conscious of the power of sin, that power which drives us to sin. But we know that such is not the case at all. The blood of the Lord Jesus has so cleansed us that our conscience no longer accuses us of our past sins. Yet this does not imply that we no longer have sin; it only affirms that there is no more consciousness of sins. Through the cleansing of the blood we are no more condemned by our conscience.

How, then, are we to be delivered from the sin that masters us, the sin which we have been speaking of in the singular number? "Knowing this, that our old man was crucified with him, that the body of sin might be done away [literally, unemployed], that so we should no longer be in bondage to sin" (Rom. 6.6). Here we have three items: (1) the body of sin, (2) the old man, and (3) sin. The body serves as a figurehead, for what causes the body to sin through the old man is sin. Sin works in the body, so that this body is called the body of sin. The old man stands between sin and the body. It accepts the instigation of sin on the one hand and directs the body to sin on the other. The old man is our personality. Sin tempts, the old man agrees, and accordingly the body acts. Some people have suggested that the death of the Lord Jesus has eradicated the root of sin. This is not true. For what the Lord Jesus has done is to get rid of the old man. Sin is still here, the body of sin is also here; only the intermediary old man is gotten rid of. Man as a person still remains; yet sin is now unable to push the new man around, because sin can never direct the new man. Sin in the singular is still here, though we are no longer in bondage to it. Why are we no longer slaves to sin? Because the old man who directly charges the body to sin is already crucified. How about the body? It is presently unemployed.

"He [the Lord Jesus] had made purification of sins" (Heb. 1.3). The sin here is again cast in the plural, for the passage points to the penalty and not to the root of sin that is purified.

Yet what about the passage in John 1.29: "Behold, the lamb of God, that taketh away the sin of the world"? Since the sin of the world which is taken away is singular in number here, does it really indicate that the root of sin is eradicated? If so, then not only the root of sin of the saved but also that of the whole world is eradicated. Obviously, this cannot be the meaning. What it means here is that the Lamb of God has solved the whole problem of the sin of the world. This agrees with the words "as through one man sin entered into the world" of Romans 5.12. Just as sin had entered into the world through one man, so it is taken away by another man. The Lord has already solved the problem of the sin of the world.

How do we deal with sin in the singular number? "Even so, reckon ye also yourselves to be dead unto sin" (Rom. 6.11). Sin in the plural is solved by the death of Christ; sin in the singular is solved by co-death with Christ. This co-death is a *reckoning* as dead. If we reckon ourselves to be dead to sin, we will no longer be under the dominion of sin.

"If we walk in the light, as he is in the light, we have fellowship one with another, and the blood of Jesus his Son cleanseth us from all sin" (1 John 1.7). Once more, the word sin is expressed in the singular. Yet this certainly cannot mean that the blood of the Lord Jesus cleanses the root of sin from us because the cleansing spoken of here is conditional on our walking in the light as He is in the light so as to have fellowship one with another. Had this verse been a reference to our sinful nature, how would we have the sin for the blood of the Lord Jesus to cleanse from us, since we are already able to walk in the light as God is in the light? The truth is: as we walk in the light of the gospel as God is in the light of revelation, we begin to realize that the blood of the Lord Jesus has already solved our whole problem of sin. In the following verse, which is the ninth verse, it uses sin in the plural, showing that we yet have sins. We therefore conclude this: that sin in the singular refers to sin as master in us, sin in the plural refers to the various expressions of outward conduct. Sin in the singular points to the whole problem of sin, while sin in the plural points to sin as individual acts.

"Him who knew no sin he made to be sin on our behalf" (2 Cor. 5.21). The word sin here is singular in form. The Lord was made sin for us, not sins (plural) on our behalf. Why is sin in the singular used here? Because God made Jesus, who knew no sin (that is, who never knew what sin was and who had never served sin nor known the power of sin), to be sin for us, that is, to be made the whole problem of sin so that God could judge it by judging Him. His being made sin simply means that God dealt with Him as God would deal with our own sin problem. If the Lord Jesus should have been made sins, He would have known sinful conduct; and thus He too would have been one who had committed sins, He too would have known sins such as pride, jealousy, uncleanness, and so on. Thank God, He had not made the Lord Jesus sins, He only dealt with the Lord Jesus as He would deal with the problem of sin. Hence when the Lord Jesus died, the problem of the sin of the whole world was solved.

Finally, let us conclude the discussion of this question by referring to the book of Romans. Its first eight chapters treat specifically the question of sin. Romans 1—5.11 is the first section, and it deals with the problem of sin in the plural number, not with sin in the singular. Romans 5.12—8 forms the second section, which deals with the problem of sin in the singular number (for please notice in the second section that, aside from the one instance in Chapter 7 where sin in the plural is mentioned, that is, verse 5, all the rest of the section speaks of sin in the singular). The first section speaks of sins as individual acts, that is, the outward expressions of sinful conduct. These sinful cases and their penalties need to be taken away and eliminated. Hence the Lord Jesus came to bear our sins and to take them away. The second section speaks of how God delivers us from the sin which reigns over us just as He has forgiven us our many sins. He not only forgives our sins and removes their penalty but also delivers us from the power of sin that we may not sin. The first section dwells on the precious blood, while the second dwells on the cross. The resurrection in the first section is the *Lord* being raised for us; the resurrection in the second is *our* being raised with the Lord. The first section focuses on the *Lord Jesus* being crucified and having shed

His blood for us; the second focuses on *our* being crucified with the Lord. The first section treats of forgiveness, the second, of deliverance. The first section deals with justification, the second, with sanctification. The first section solves the penalty of sin, the second dissolves the power of sin. We need to pass through both of these two sections.

When you first believe in the Lord, you are worried about the many sins you have committed. One sin after another is laid before you, and you realize that there is nothing good within and without you. You begin to wonder how the all-just God could forgive your sins. But as you come to know that the Lord Jesus has borne your sins, that His blood has cleansed you of all your sins, and that He has forgiven you of all the sins you committed, you rejoice in Him. Having had your sins forgiven you now stand in the grace of God, expecting joyously the glory of God. You are fully persuaded that you now can do good.

Yet day by day you discover that, for example, you can still lie as you did before. What should be done? You come to the Lord, asking for forgiveness. The Lord is still willing to forgive, and His blood is always efficacious. You make up your mind that you will never lie again. You subsequently seem to do all right during the first few days, but then you begin to relax, and once more you lie. Again you ask the Lord to forgive your sin, and again you will not to sin. After a while, you lie once more and fall. Again and again you ask the Lord to forgive you, and over and over again you sin. Formerly you felt the sinfulness of outward sins; now, after you have become a Christian, you are aware of the sin that reigns within you as well as the sins committed without. To illustrate further, let us consider the person who loves to gamble. Formerly he acknowledged this as a defect in his conduct. But after he has believed in the Lord, he begins to sense that there is a hard master in him who has the power to force him to do what he does not want to do and he cannot but do it.

Each of us has his own peculiar sin which entangles him. You may recall how happy you were at the time you were saved, but now you are even more miserable than before you were saved. How can you overcome these sins? You inquire of God if He has a greater salvation. That which is described in Romans 5.12 to 8 is that greater salvation. If blood is all that God requires, He could cause the Lord Jesus to shed His blood in a different way. Why must Christ die on the cross? It is because God wants to show you how as a person you were brought to the cross to be crucified with Christ just as the penalty of your sinful acts of conduct was pardoned through Jesus the Savior. The Lord Jesus Christ was crucified for your sins, but at the same time He brought you to the cross with Him. Not only the sins of the sinner, but also the sinner himself; not just our sins, but also all of us in Christ, were on the cross. Just as the Lord Jesus Christ has shed His blood to cleanse your sins, so God has reckoned Christ's death over 1900 years ago as being your death.

At the beginning you believed that the Lord has died for you; today you reckon His death as your death. Since the Lord has died, you too have died. As you believe in His death, so you also believe His death as your death. Though sin is still alive it cannot tempt a dead person, because he who is dead is freed from sin. The person being dead, sin can no longer baffle him. God can forgive our outward sinful acts of conduct, but He cannot forgive our inward sinful nature. Instead, He has crucified our old man so that sin in us has no more power to drag us down. We must therefore believe that we were dead. Believe that we already died, not that we are going to die. Believe that we have died, not that we should die. When you are conscious of your weakness and uncleanness, you should know that the cross has already dealt with these things. If you look at Christ with believing eyes and believe that you have been crucified with Him, you will see the power of Christ in saving and delivering you from the power of sin in you.

The first step in salvation gives us peace and satisfaction and causes us to experience much joy. The second step in salvation gives us power to overcome sin and to walk in His way. Do you sense the power of sin oppressing you within? It is well that you experience the victory over it. Overcoming the power of sin in you is deliverance and emancipation, not forgiveness. Since the master within you has been changed, you are no longer under the rule of the old master. We must all go this way.

Question 8

Are we saved by the grace of God or by the righteousness of God? Which part of salvation is done for us by God's grace, and which part of it by God's righteousness?

Answer:

"By grace have ye been saved" (Eph. 2.8), thus indicating that we are saved by grace.

"Christ Jesus: whom God set forth to be a propitiation [literally, mercy seat], through faith, in his blood, to show his righteousness . . . ; for the showing, I say, of his righteousness at this present season: that he might himself be just, and the justifier of him that hath faith in Jesus"

(Rom. 3.24–26), thus signifying that we are also saved by God's righteousness.

The grace of God provides for us a Savior that we may be saved (see John 3.16). The righteousness of God causes salvation to come upon us, for He cannot but save us. That part of God's provision which extends from the birth of the Lord Jesus to His death and resurrection is done for us through God's grace. And the part from the ascension of the Lord Jesus to the present moment is done for us through God's righteousness.

Grace may be given or withheld according to God's pleasure; but righteousness must be dispensed without favor. Since Christ has died and been raised from the dead, God cannot but save me if I believe. Otherwise, God would be found to be unrighteous. How does 1 John 1.9 read? Does it say: "If we confess our sins, he is merciful and loving to forgive us our sins, and to cleanse us from all unrighteousness"? No, it says that "he is *faithful* and *righteous* . . ." The blood of God's Son has already cleansed us from all our sins. As we believe, God must save us. God cannot be unfaithful, because His word has already been spoken. He cannot be unrighteous, because the blood of His Son has already been shed. We thank and praise God, for He cannot but save us!

Whatever is unrighteous is sin. God cannot be unrighteous, hence He cannot but save us. Suppose we say that God may or may not forgive us. This would almost be like saying that He is unfaithful and unrighteous. Let us lay hold of God's righteousness. How God is pleased indeed with our laying hold of His righteousness! For to lay hold of His righteousness is truly honoring Him.

Question 9

Which saves us: the righteousness of God (see Rom.
3.21–26) or the righteousness of Christ? What are their
meanings and differences?

Answer:

It is the righteousness of God which saves us.

What is the righteousness of God? "Whom [i.e., Christ
Jesus] God set forth to be a propitiation [literally, mercy
seat], through faith, in his blood, to show his righteousness
because of the passing over of the sins done aforetime, in the
forbearance of God; for the showing, I say, of his righteousness at this present season: that he might himself be just,
and the justifier of him that hath faith in Jesus" (Rom.
3.25,26). The mercy seat sits on the Ark; it is where God
meets with men. God has set forth Jesus as the mercy seat,
which is to say that He can only communicate in Christ
with men. Had there been no mercy seat on the Ark, the
law in the Ark would have condemned man's sin. But with
the blood on the mercy seat, the law could no longer
condemn the sin of man, because its demand has already
been met. Thus is manifested the righteousness of God,
which means that God is just.

According to the law, he who sins must die. Since the
Lord Jesus has died for us, we do not need to die. Hence
forgiveness is given according to the righteousness of God.
Suppose, for example, that someone owes you a hundred
dollars and he gives you an I O U note. As soon as he pays
you back the hundred dollars, you should return the note to
him so as to conclude the debt. But if you refuse to return
the note, and yet still press him for payment, you are an

unrighteous person. I have sinned and I deserve to die. But I have availed myself of the blood of Christ to repay my sinful debt. God cannot require anything from me any further. For this reason, the forgiveness of my sins is according to the righteousness of God. Under all circumstances, then, God must forgive us because the Lord Jesus has died for us.

"If we confess our sins, he is faithful and righteous to forgive us our sins, and to cleanse us from all unrighteousness" (1 John 1.9). God's being "faithful" here is in regard to His own word: whatever God says is firmly established. And His being "righteous" is in relation to the accomplished work of Christ: Christ having met all God's demands for us, God will require nothing of us any more. His word declares that he who believes is forgiven; we believe, therefore God must forgive us. Christ has died and God's demand is thereby fully met, so He must forgive. In the passing over of the sins done aforetime and in justifying —at this present season—all who believe, God manifests himself as just.

God has not only justified us, He also has convinced us that He is just. He is just in treating us in the way He has done. Jesus is a man, we too are human beings. Now just as sin entered into the world through one man, so it is to be taken away through one man. When Adam sinned, it was more than a personal matter; it became a concern for all mankind: for Adam is the head, and we all are parts of him. But so likewise are we in Christ: when Christ died, we all too died; and when Christ was resurrected, life flows into us. There is no need for us to implore God plaintively for forgiveness. Christ has already died for us, so God cannot but forgive us. If we believe, we shall be saved.

Nowhere in the whole New Testament can a single verse be found affirming that the righteousness of Christ saves us. For the righteousness of Christ is solely used to qualify Christ himself to be the Savior. The righteousness of Christ refers to His own good conduct. He saves us by His death, not by His righteousness. His death fulfills the righteousness of God. His righteousness is like the veil in the tabernacle made of four different colors. He alone can see God, all others are kept away outside the veil. When the veil is rent (that is, when Christ has died), a new and living way is opened for us that we may draw nigh to God (Heb. 10.20,22).

How, then, are we to explain 1 Corinthians 1.30 which says that Christ Jesus "was made unto us . . . from God . . . righteousness" and 1 Peter 3.18 which mentions "the righteous for the unrighteous"? Is the righteousness of Christ actually being mentioned in these two places? Not at all. For in 1 Corinthians 1 it is Christ *himself* who is made our righteousness, and in 1 Peter 3 it is Christ *himself* being righteous who is qualified to be a substitute for us who are unrighteous.

As regards 2 Peter 1.1—which reads: "Simon Peter, a servant and apostle of Jesus Christ, to them that have obtained like precious faith with us in the righteousness of our God and the Savior Jesus Christ"—the "righteousness" here may be translated as "justness" or "fairness", thus signifying that He is not partial to anyone since He gives the same precious faith to the latecomers as well as to the firstcomers, to the Gentiles as well as to the Jews (see Acts 10.34,45; 15.8,9,11).

Question 10

What is the difference between the righteousness of Christ and Christ as righteousness?

Answer:

Christ as righteousness is found in 1 Corinthians 1.30: "Of him [God] are ye in Christ Jesus, who was made unto us wisdom from God, and righteousness and sanctification, and redemption"; this verse tells us that God has made Christ to be our righteousness.

The righteousness of Christ is Christ's good conduct while on earth as a man. It is His personal earthly virtue. But Christ as righteousness is this: that God has given Him to us to be our righteousness. The righteousness of Christ refers to His own goodness, while Christ as righteousness refers to His own Self.

The righteousness of Christ is likened to the meal-offering numbered among the five offerings. There is no blood in the meal-offering because it typifies the earthly life—with its good deeds and virtues—of our Lord Jesus. But Christ as righteousness may be likened to the burnt-offering. As it is an offering of a sweet savor to God, it typifies Christ as being accepted by God. With Christ as our righteousness, we offer Him up as we draw nigh to God, thus being accepted by God even as Christ is accepted. God will look upon us as being as perfect as Christ. On the other hand, the sin-offering signifies how Christ is offered up to atone for the sin of our entire life, and the trespass-offering is offered up to atone for our daily sins. Both of these deal with the matter of sin. Burnt-offering, however, is for God to be able to look upon us as being as good as Christ. In the Old Testament there is a term called "Jehovah our righteousness" (Jer. 33.16). This is to say that God himself is ours. Having Christ as our righteousness, we can answer all of God's demands which had been placed upon us.

Question 11

What does the persecution which the Lord Jesus suffered signify? And what does the death of the Lord Jesus signify?

Answer:

The persecution of the Lord Jesus expresses the love of God, and the death of the Lord Jesus expresses the righteousness of God.

If the earthly life of our Lord Jesus had only manifested righteousness, He would not have encountered so much opposition. We need to see that His receiving the tax-collectors and sinners showed forth love, not righteousness. And for this the Pharisees criticized Him (Matt. 9.11). Because He healed the sick on the Sabbath day, the Pharisees took counsel against Him to destroy Him (Matt. 12.10–14). Note His answer to the disciples of John: "Go and tell John the things which ye hear and see: the blind receive their sight, and the lame walk, the lepers are cleansed, and the deaf hear, and the dead are raised up, and the poor have good tidings preached to them. And blessed is he, whosoever shall find no occasion of stumbling in me" (Matt. 11.4–6). Whatever the Lord had done here was grace. Yet He was afraid lest people would stumble over such abundant grace, and hence He added, "Blessed is he, whosoever shall find no occasion of stumbling."

Once He spoke to the people at Nazareth, saying, "There were many widows in Israel in the days of Elijah, when the heaven was shut up three years and six months, when there came a great famine over all the land; and unto none of them was Elijah sent, but only to Zarephath, in the land of Sidon, unto a woman that was a widow. And there were many lepers in Israel in the time of Elisha the prophet; and none of them was cleansed, but only Naaman the Syrian" (Luke 4.25–27). This too expresses love, for a widow is most pitiful and the Gentiles are looked down upon by the Jews. As they heard these things, those in the synagogue were all filled with wrath. They rose up and cast Him forth out of the city. They led Him to the brow of a hill that they might throw Him down headlong. It may therefore be said that the Lord suffered immense persecution throughout His life. This was due to the fact that whatever He did was expressive of the love of God.

The death of the Lord, though, expresses the righteousness of God. Because there on the cross the Lord bore the sin of the entire world and suffered the judgment of God in order to fulfill all the demands of the law.

How we thank the Lord that He becomes the sinner's friend before He is the sinner's Savior. He first loves us and so works in us that we may believe and receive the redemption which He has accomplished on the cross.

Question 12

Why is it that in God's plan of redemption Christ must be simultaneously God and man?

Answer:

Suppose there are three persons, A, B, and C. C has sinned, and A asks B to die for C. In so doing, A is able to express his love for C, and C is also able to answer the demand of the law, but all this will be rather unjust to B. I have sinned, and God causes Christ to die for me. Thus is manifested the love of God toward me, and in addition I have met the requirement of the law. Yet will it not be highly unrighteous to Christ? Only when Christ is both man and God at the same time can it be truly just.

First of all, then, we need to know what is forgiveness. To forgive presupposes a loss to the forgiver through the offense of the forgiven. For instance, if someone owes you ten dollars and you forgive him, it automatically means that you suffer the loss of ten dollars.

In God's plan of redemption, Christ should not be a third party. If He be a third party, God would be being unjust to Christ since Christ has no sin and hence is not subject to death. The Bible tells us that men have sinned and God is offended. So what is involved is the relation between God and men. To ask a third party to die as a substitute may perhaps fulfill the law's demand on men as well as fulfill God's righteousness, but this will be most unjust to that third party. Only because Christ is simultaneously God and man can this substitution be termed just.

"Wherewith shall I come before Jehovah, and bow myself before the high God? shall I come before him with burnt-offerings, with calves a year old? will Jehovah be pleased with thousands of rams, or with ten thousands of rivers of oil? shall I give my first-born for my transgression, the fruit of my body for the sin of my soul?" (Micah 6.6,7) Here it is stated that if we sin against God, it is futile to offer calves and rams. All kinds of offerings are of no avail, not even the firstborn ones of our bodies. Christ, therefore, must be God who is himself being offended. For only in this way will He not become a third party. Because Christ is God, the work of redemption is justified. Stating it conversely, since the work of redemption is just, Christ must be God, since only the offended can ever forgive the offender. Who can ever then say that forgiveness is unrighteous? Because Christ is God and He is the One being sinned against, He is therefore able to forgive us.

Consider these two verses: "The commandment, which was unto life, this I found to be unto death" (Rom. 7.10); "The wages of sin is death" (6.23). These passages cause us to see that unless a person keeps all the laws perfectly he must die. In order to make us live, the Lord himself needs to suffer the penalty of sin, which is death. Nevertheless, it is said in 1 Timothy 6.16 that God "[alone] hath immortality"; and hence, for Christ to die as our substitute He must simultaneously be man. And in His body as a man He died for us. So that we can rightly say this: He is God, therefore He has the possibility of saving men.

Question 13

Why does Romans 5.18 say "one (act)" and 5.19 say "one (man)"?

Answer:

Let us first dissect Romans 5.12–21. Verses 13–17 serve as a footnote or a kind of parenthetical explanation to verse 12, so verse 18 should follow closely upon verse 12. Let us first proceed with verse 12.

"Therefore, as through one man sin entered into the world, and death through sin; and so death passed unto all men, for that all sinned" (Rom. 5.12). Adam is like a channel through which the sin in him flows into the world.

And death trails after sin. Death thus passes not only to one man but to all men because all have sinned. But after Paul had written this verse, he perhaps feared that someone might raise the following questions: Since there was no law in Adam's time, where did sin come from? And if there were no sin, how could there be death? Paul therefore puts in a parenthetical explanation, verses 13 to 17, which may be subdivided into three sections.

"For until the law sin was in the world; but sin is not imputed when there is no law. Nevertheless death reigned from Adam until Moses, even over them that had not sinned after the likeness of Adam's transgression, who is a figure of him that was to come" (vv.13,14). What Paul means is that indeed sin is not imputed when there is no law, yet this does not signify that because there is no law sin is not there. Paul deals with fact—namely, that though there was no law, sin was already in the world. For since there was obviously death in the world, there must also be sin in the world. As all died, death had passed to all men, for all had sinned. And even though not all had sinned after the likeness of Adam's transgression, even so, all came under death. Paul tries to prove one thing, which is, that although it is something perpetrated by this one man, Adam, it nevertheless affects the whole of mankind. Not only Adam himself receives the consequence of it, all the rest of mankind receives the same consequence too. And just as this is true with Adam, it is likewise true with Christ. What Christ has done influences the whole world, since Adam is a figure of Christ.

"But not as the trespass, so also is the free gift. For if by the trespass of the one the many died, much more did the grace of God, and the gift by the grace of the one man, Jesus Christ, abound unto the many" (v.15). This verse compares the nature of trespass with that of the gift of grace. The trespass is not as the free gift. The reason Paul gives for this is that since Adam's transgression has caused all to die, will not the gift of God's grace abound to the many? What kind of grace is the grace of God? The grace of God which comes freely through one man, Jesus Christ, will surely abound to the many.

"And not as through one that sinned, so is the gift; for the judgment came of one unto condemnation, but the free gift came of many trespasses unto justification. For if, by the trespass of the one, death reigned through the one; much more shall they that receive the abundance of grace and of the gift of righteousness reign in life through the one, even Jesus Christ" (vv.16,17). These two verses make a comparison between the consequence (or recompense) of trespass and the consequence of free gift. As regards the consequence, the trespass is again not as the free gift. Because of the transgression of one man, God, according to righteousness, judges not only the one man but also the many. The one man's transgression results in the many being condemned. What, though, about free gift? It forgives many trespasses—not just the one trespass, but the many trespasses. Hence the consequence of free gift far surpasses that of trespass. If one transgression can affect so many people, what will be the degree of condemnation should there be ten or a hundred transgressions? Even so, the gift of God can forgive even this much trespass and more. Its effect is far more excellent indeed. Verse 17 thus reinforces verse 16 by stating that, having both grace and righteousness, surely we may reign in life.

"So then as through one trespass the judgment came unto all men to condemnation; even so through one act of righteousness the free gift came unto all men to justification of life" (v.18). This verse 18, as was indicated earlier, follows closely upon the text of verse 12. In verse 12 it is said that, through the transgression of the one man Adam, death passes to all men since all have sinned. Here in verse 18 it is continued with, "so then as through one trespass . . . all men to condemnation; even so through one act of righteousness . . . all men to justification of life": for the one trespass of Adam, all are condemned; and similarly, for the one act of righteousness of Christ (having fulfilled righteousness by being crucified once on the cross), all are justified unto life.

If anyone does not accept this teaching, it will be hard for him to acknowledge himself as a sinner. For the Bible does not say that one becomes a sinner after he has sinned, rather does it say that all men are by very nature sinners. If you are a human, you are a sinner. The reason for our being sinners is because Adam sinned. Many are unclear about the salvation of Christ due to their lack of understanding about Adam. If you can see that in Adam all are condemned, you will have no trouble in seeing that in Christ all are justified to life.

Thanks and praise be to God, for what we obtain in Christ is much more than what we lost in Adam. We are sinners because of the one transgression of Adam; we may be saved because of the one act of righteousness of Christ. The one trespass of Adam produces such a consequence, yet how much better a consequence is brought in by the one act of the righteousness of Christ.

"For as through the one man's disobedience the many were made sinners, even so through the obedience of the one shall the many be made righteous" (v.19). This verse explains that the reason for this better consequence lies in this Man being better than the other man. To put it the other way around, the first instance is not as the second instance simply because the first man is not as the second

Man. For example: A and B are sweeping the floor. A does not sweep as well as B, because A as a person is inferior to B as a person. Verse 18 declares that what Adam once did is far less than what Christ has done. Verse 19 tells us the reason for such a contrast: Adam as a man is so much inferior to Christ as a man. Adam disobeyed, but Christ has obeyed. As through the disobedience of the one man Adam the many were constituted sinners, so through the obedience of the one man Christ shall the many be constituted righteous.

"And the law came in besides, that the trespass might abound; but where sin abounded, grace did abound more exceedingly" (v.20). The law does not cause trespass to abound, it only makes manifest more trespasses. It does not drive people to sin, it merely exposes men's sins—just as a mirror reveals the dirty spots on my face, although it adds no further dirty spots to my face. The law comes in besides to show us what great sinners we are. As soon as we begin to know ourselves we will be shown by God how His grace surpasses sin.

"That, as sin reigned in death, even so might grace reign through righteousness unto eternal life through Jesus Christ our Lord" (v.21). Adam has passed away, and now the gospel is present. Thanks be to God, our salvation does not depend on us. This is the gospel.

Question 14

Did Christ keep the law for us? Is there any direct relationship between our salvation and His keeping the law?

Answer:

Christ's keeping the law gives Him the righteousness which qualifies Him to be the Savior. Consequently, Christ's keeping the law has only an indirect relationship to our salvation.

Christ saves us by His death—He suffered for us the penalty imposed by the law. He does not save us by His keeping the law. It is the death of Christ that saves us; it is the righteousness which He fulfills by His death, not the righteousness which He has in life. His personal righteousness is all for His own Self.

Question 15

How do we establish the law through faith (Rom. 3.31)? Why are believers not under law (Rom. 6.14)? What is meant by not being under the law? Why is Christ the end of the law (Rom. 10.4)?

Answer:

"Do we then make the law of none effect through faith? God forbid: nay, we establish the law" (Rom. 3.31). This is a judgment made by Paul. Since he has maintained earlier that "we reckon therefore that a man is justified by faith apart from the works of the law" (v.28), he may legitimately be asked the question—"Do we then make the law of none effect through faith?" His answer is emphatically, No. Here he employs a Greek form of speech: God forbid! By which he means to say that even *God* forbid us to say that we make the law of none effect through faith.

In the first three chapters of Romans Paul shows us that even as the Gentiles whom God has not chosen are sinners, so the Jews whom God *has* chosen are sinners too—that even those who serve God and have the law of God are also sinners. Therefore, no one is justified by the works of the law, "because by the works of the law shall no flesh be justified in his sight; for through the law cometh the knowledge of sin" (3.20).

"But now apart from the law a righteousness of God hath been manifested, being witnessed by the law and the prophets" (3.21). Praise and thank God, there is a "but now". Now is there a salvation.

"[Christ Jesus] whom God set forth to be a propitiation, through faith, in his blood, to show his righteousness because of the passing over of the sins done aforetime, in the forbearance of God; for the showing, I say, of his righteousness at this present season: that he might himself be just, and the justifier of him that hath faith in Jesus" (3.25,26). In relation to the people in the Old Testament dispensation God forbears; in relation to the people in this present dispensation He justifies. During the old dispensation the Lord has yet to die and sin has not been taken away, so God forbears with men. Today God justifies us, not just forbears with us. To be justified means more than being forgiven or not reckoned as sinful; it means being counted as righteous. And God gives us this righteousness in Christ Jesus. Because of the death and resurrection of Christ, we come into possession of this righteousness. For this reason, says Paul, "we reckon therefore that a man is justified by faith apart from the works of the law" (v.28). Still, being afraid that some people may assume from this that faith abrogates the law, Paul immediately adds, "God forbid".

How, then, do we establish the law through faith? The law has made only two demands: (1) the law commands all to do good, and (2) the law penalizes those who do not do good. The law must be fulfilled in either of them. If you do not keep the law, you will suffer the penalty of the law. If you fail to establish the law by observing it, you will have to take its penalty to establish it. Apart from the Lord there is not a single person who can keep the law. Even Moses the lawgiver has not wholly kept it. The law demands for all who do not keep it to die. We confess that we have not kept the law and that we have sinned, but we declare that we have already died. Since in Christ we have already been judged and cursed by the law, we have not destroyed the law, but rather, that through faith we have established it. Although we are unable to establish the law by keeping it and therefore we must die, thank God, we have already died in Christ! "But of him [God] are ye in Christ Jesus" (1 Cor. 1.30). It is God who puts us in Christ. When Christ died, we too have died in His death. Consequently, faith has not destroyed the law but instead has established it.

Why are believers not under law? Believers are not under law because (1) they have already died, and (2) they have also been resurrected. This is proven by Romans 7.1–6. Paul chooses the parable of a woman with her husband. At the outset, let us determine who is the "husband" in this passage. Some say the husband is the law, while others say the husband is our flesh. These two schools of opinion have their respective reasons. By reading the passage carefully we may see that actually both thoughts are included. In verse 2 we are shown first that the husband is the law, but then it also shows us that the husband is different from the law. So the husband in this passage means either the law or the flesh. Should the husband represent merely the law then the clause, "if the husband die", will mean "if the law die". But how can the law die? For this reason, we conclude that the husband here may point to either the flesh or the law.

Before one believes in the Lord he is bound by the law. How can he be delivered? Only through death. If he dies he is freed. Once he dies he is freed from the law. God has already condemned sin in the flesh of Christ. Since we have died in Christ we are freed from the law. You are like a woman, and your flesh is like the husband. As you die you are freed from the flesh. The most the law can demand is death. No matter how many sins a criminal has committed, the law can at the most condemn him to but one death. Once he dies the case is concluded. When we die we are freed from the law.

On the other hand, it is said that "if the husband die, she is discharged from the law of the husband". This terminates your relationship with the law. You are discharged from the law as though by death. The first half of the sentence emphasizes death, whereas the second half of the sentence stresses deliverance.

This same passage also shows us two pictures: one indicates that through the body of Christ I am dead to the law, being wholly freed from the law. On that day when Christ died, I too died. Thus I can say to the law: I am not under law. The other picture indicates that I now may be remarried. Formerly the flesh was my husband, but now I am remarried to the Christ who has been raised from the dead so that I may bring forth fruit to God. Hence no Christian is today under law.

Should anyone tell you: "You must keep the law, you must keep the Sabbath day", you ought to realize that if you try to keep one single item in the book of law you unwittingly declare that Christ has not died for you, and therefore you cast away the work of Christ. Let us compare the words in Romans 6.14 with 3.19—"Sin shall not have dominion over you: for ye are not under law, but under grace." This indicates that believers are not under law. But to whom do the things of the law speak? "Now we know that what things soever the law saith, it speaketh to them that are under the law; that every mouth may be stopped, and all the world may be brought under the judgment of God." The things of the law speak to those who are under the law. Since we Christians are not under law, these things of the law do not speak to us.

Why does Paul write the Galatian letter after he has written his letter to the Romans? Romans informs us that no sinner can be justified by keeping the law; Galatians instructs us that no saint may be sanctified by works of the law. Not only a sinner cannot be saved by works, even a saint cannot be sanctified by works. Just as one begins in grace, so he shall be perfected through grace. How can he who is justified by faith ever imagine himself to be sanctified by keeping the law? If justification is by the Holy Spirit, sanctification must also be by the Holy Spirit. The way of completion is the way of entry, for God has only one working principle. Why is it forbidden to weave together wool and linen (Deut. 22.11)? Because wool is obtained through the shedding of blood, whereas linen comes from man's planting. Whatever is done by God is God's work; whatever is done by man is man's work. God will not mix up His work with man's work.

What is meant by not being under law? *Not to be under law does not mean lawlessness.* The Bible says: "Sin shall not have dominion over you: for ye are not under law, but under grace" (Rom. 6.14). You are not under law, because you are under grace. Being under grace, you will not be ruled by sin. We need to pay special attention to this word.

Not to be under law does not sanction licentiousness; it only means that sin shall not have dominion over you.

What is meant by being under grace? "If it is by grace, it is no more of works: otherwise grace is no more grace" (Rom. 11.6). To be under grace simply means you need not have your own works. What then is meant by being under law? It means you yourself should do the works even though the more you work the worse you become. Being under grace means that the Lord Jesus is doing all; being under law is, you yourself doing all. In being under grace, God so works in you that sin shall have no more dominion over you; in being under law, you are under the dominion of sin because you cannot overcome it. If you are under grace, the grace of God will work in you. Is sin, then, any match for God's grace? Certainly not.

As the Lord Jesus has died for you on the cross, even so today He lives in you. As He has borne your sins on the cross, so now He dwells in you to give you victory over sin. The law is only God's commandment; but grace is the power of God. The law commands you to do, but grace gives you the power to do it. Not to be under law but to be under grace means the risen Christ lives in you and causes you to overcome.

Why is Christ the end of the law? This is because Christ has satisfied all the demands of the law laid upon men.

We must see first of all that Christ in His life sums up the law. Leaving totally aside the aspect of the Lord Jesus as God, let us dwell for a moment on the aspect of His being man. There is only one human being in the whole world who has kept the law completely—and that person is the Lord Jesus. There is none other before Him nor any other after Him. He alone possesses the qualification. He is therefore the sum of the law.

Secondly, the death of Christ concludes the law. The last and highest of its demands is death. Suppose, for example, that a person sinned against the law of a country and was then condemned to be shot. After he is shot, the law of the country can do no more to him. The law can only demand death, and in death everything is solved. The law says that whoever does not keep the law must die. But the Lord Jesus has died, and by that death He concludes the law.

"End" means that which is "final". What can be added after the final thing has been reached? What more can be done afterward? Consequently, let every Christian give praise to God, knowing that Christ has already concluded the law.

Question 16

How does Christ fulfill the law and the prophets (Matt. 5.17)?

Answer:

In order to answer this question, let us read carefully Matthew 5.17–20.

Let us first consider the words "Think not" in the verse which reads, "Think not that I came to destroy the law or the prophets: I came not to destroy, but to fulfil" (v.17). Why does the Lord say this? Because there is the possibility of so thinking, that perhaps some of His hearers are thinking in this very way. The Lord has just announced the nine beatitudes, but He then talks about two more matters:

(1) you are the salt of the earth, and (2) you are the light of the world. As the people present hear these things, they may probably think how completely contrary what the Lord is saying today as being blessed is to the Old Covenant conception of what is blessed. According to the Old Covenant God makes Israel great, and causes the Israelites to destroy their enemies. But today the Lord speaks of humility, gentleness, persecution, and so on—things which are so totally foreign to the Old Covenant concept. Does the Lord therefore come to destroy the law? Formerly God had put Israel on earth to be a testimony, but now He transfers this testimony to a few among the children of Israel and calls them the salt and the light. Does He not therefore indeed come to destroy the law? Hence immediately after He has finished saying you are the salt and the light, He continues with "Think not". He clarifies further by saying, "I came not to destroy, but to fulfil". The word "destroy" in the original Greek has in it the picture of tearing down a wall piece by piece, whereas the word "fulfil" in the original means to fill to the full.

As regards the attitude of the Lord Jesus toward the law, there are two different ancient views. One view is held by those who assert that to fulfill the law the Lord Jesus destroys the law. They argue that what the Lord says here differs greatly from what Moses said. Moses declared, for instance, that "whosoever shall put away his wife, let him give her a writing of divorcement", but the Lord declares that "every one that putteth away his wife, saving for the cause of fornication, maketh her an adulteress" (Matt. 5.31,32). In their view, therefore, the Lord opposes Moses. The other view is that the Lord comes to preserve the purity of the law by destroying all which the Jews have added on to the law of Moses during the 1500 years preceding Jesus. We believe, however, that fulfill means what it says: to fill to the full; and that hence it cannot be explained by either of these two views. We will now try to explain what the Lord's attitude really is toward the law.

First of all, the Lord acknowledges that the law and the prophets come from God. By saying, "for so persecuted they the prophets that were before you" (Matt. 5.12), He recognizes the prophets as being of God. Moreover, by mentioning the offering of a gift at the altar, He thereby exhibits no opposition to the altar. And, furthermore, after He had finished the teaching on the mount, He came down and met a leper whom He cleansed. Whereupon He immediately commanded the leper who was cleansed to show himself to the priests and offer the gift prescribed by Moses (Matt. 8.1–4). All these instances indicate that the Lord admits to everything which Moses had commanded must be done.

Second, although the Lord acknowledges that the law and the prophets do indeed come from God, He nonetheless also informs us that the law is not complete. In the fifth chapter of Matthew we read again and again the words: "Ye have heard that it was said . . . : but I say unto you". What the Lord means is that while it is right for Moses to say "thou shalt not kill" and "thou shalt not commit adultery", He must tell us that these are incomplete since it is wrong even to get angry without cause and even to lust after a woman. Let us clearly understand that to say that something is incomplete is not to say that it is bad. For example, when a child begins to learn the simple addition of two plus two makes four, so far as knowledge goes, what he has learned is incomplete but certainly it is not something bad.

Third, the Lord comes to fill up what the law lacks. "Fulfil" points to the Lord's filling full as the Teacher, not as the Savior. This is to say that where the law is lacking, at that very point the Lord fills it up to fullness. The law teaches an eye for an eye and a tooth for a tooth—which is the principle of fairness or righteousness. The Lord, however, instructs us to love our enemies and pray for them who persecute us—and this is the principle of grace. The law manifests the way God works as characterized by justice, but grace and mercy express the very nature of God himself. According to the grace of the Lord, God makes His sun to rise on the evil and the good and sends rain on the just and on the unjust. "For the law was given through Moses; grace and truth came through Jesus Christ" (John 1.17). Moses tells us of God's way of doing things, whereas the Lord tells us of the very nature of God.

Since the Lord has already suffered the curse of the law on the cross in our stead, we who have accepted the Lord's work on the cross and thereby received life ought to live on earth according to all which on the mount He has commanded us to do. Some people suggest that what the Lord has spoken on the mount is law and not grace; therefore, the teaching on the mount is directed to the Jews. There are several proofs to demonstrate the error of such a view.

First, according to proper reasoning, we should not push all the hard things onto the Jews while leaving the easy things for ourselves. Just consider for a moment the illogic of such a position: Would God require more from the Jews to whom He has granted less power and grace and require less from us who have received more power and grace?

Second, it is distinctly stated in Matthew 5.1,2 that in this event on the mount the Lord was speaking to the disciples. If, as some intimate, the disciples here point to the Jews, then there is at least one Bible verse which declares that the disciples are Christians (Acts 11.26) but that nowhere in the Bible does it say that "the disciples are

Jews", nor is there to be found in the Scriptures such a term as "Jewish disciple". As soon as one becomes a disciple, there is no longer the distinction between Jew and Gentile.

Third, it is stated in Matthew 28: "Go ye therefore, and make disciples of all the nations, baptizing them into the name of the Father and of the Son and of the Holy Spirit: teaching them to observe all things whatsoever I commanded you" (vv.19,20). When we preach the gospel we must at the same time teach people to observe the teachings of the Lord which no doubt include the teaching on the mount. Admittedly, the teaching on the mount is hard, but we cannot arbitrarily push that which is difficult onto the Jews. "The Comforter, even the Holy Spirit, whom the Father will send in my name, he shall teach you all things, and bring to your remembrance all that I said unto you" (John 14.26). Notice the clause "all that I said unto you"—signifying not just a believing unto eternal life but including all the commands of the Lord. The work which the Holy Spirit comes to do is to cause people to observe everything which the Lord has taught and commanded. The apostles are charged with the responsibility of teaching people to observe the teachings of the Lord as well as with that of preaching the gospel.

"For verily I say unto you, Till heaven and earth pass away, one jot or one tittle shall in no wise pass away from the law, till all things be accomplished" (Matt. 5.18). Jot is the smallest letter in the Hebrew alphabet, tittle is the little turn of the stroke by which one letter differs from another similar to it. To indicate that each jot and tittle is to be fulfilled is to say that all things shall be accomplished. The heaven and the earth will not pass away till all the jots and all the tittles of the law have been accomplished.

In verse 17 we have the law and the prophets, but in verse 18 only the law. Why is this so? Because the law speaks as far as to the millennium, whereas some prophets prophesy to eternity (Isaiah, for example, mentions the *new* heaven and the *new* earth). Should heaven and earth pass away before all things which the prophets have said are accomplished, then those matters spoken of in the book of Revelation will be turned upside down. How our Lord weighs every word—no more, no less! He has said that heaven and earth shall in no wise pass away till every jot and tittle of the law be accomplished. How solemn and full of dignity is the law.

One time Jesus said to a lawyer of the Pharisees: "Thou shalt love the Lord thy God with all thy heart, and with all thy soul, and with all thy mind. This is the great and first commandment. And a second like unto it is this, Thou shalt love thy neighbor as thyself. On these two commandments the whole law hangeth, and the prophets" (Matt. 22.37–40). He also said to the Pharisees: "I desire mercy, and not sacrifice" (Matt. 9.13). The Lord shows us here that moral law is more important than all other laws. "Woe unto you, scribes and Pharisees, hypocrites! for ye tithe mint and anise and cummin, and have left undone the weightier matters of the law, justice, and mercy, and faith: but these ye ought to have done, and not to have left the other undone" (Matt. 23.23). Here the Lord indicates the more and the less important in the law. Some may have observed in quite a complete manner all which was on the ceremonial side of the law, but the Lord still chides them. The tithing of mint and anise and cummin, not weaving wool and linen together, not cooking the lamb in its milk, and so forth belong to those commandments of the law which were of secondary importance.

Must we Christians also keep the law? No, because Christians are not under law but under grace (Rom. 6.14). During the apostolic age, a few taught the brethren saying,

Unless you are circumcised according to Mosaic law you cannot be saved (see Acts 15.5). In reply Peter said, "Now therefore why make ye trial of God, that ye should put a yoke upon the neck of the disciples which neither our fathers nor we were able to bear?" (v.10) Finally, the apostles and the elders in Jerusalem wrote a letter to the brethren who were of the Gentiles, admonishing them to abstain from the pollution of idols and from fornication and from what is strangled and from blood, without requiring them to be circumcised (vv.22–29).

On the other hand, while the Lord was still on earth and before His death and resurrection, and although He was the meaning of all these ceremonial laws, He and His disciples nevertheless kept the law (recall, for example, how both Peter and the Lord paid the temple tax, Matt. 17.24–27). The law continued in force until the death of the Lord. But at the Lord's death all these ceremonial laws were fulfilled and thus passed away. We must notice the dispensational relationship here.

After the coming of the Holy Spirit and the establishing of the church, Peter still desired to keep the ceremonial law in the case of not eating the unclean creatures mentioned in Leviticus 11. How did God instruct him? "What God hath cleansed, make not thou common" (see Acts 10.9–15). There is thus a change under the New Covenant. In the Letter to the Galatians Paul, in speaking about circumcision (which was the most important law to the Jews), most earnestly declared: "Behold, I Paul say unto you, that, if ye receive circumcision, Christ will profit you nothing. Yea, I testify again to every man that receiveth circumcision, that he is a debtor to do the whole law" (Gal. 5.2,3). Paul shows us here the entire law. For unless you keep all the laws, you do not keep any one law. You cannot keep only that which you desire and reject those which you do not desire. Here, then, can we be clear that we are not under law.

The "kingdom" in Matthew 5.19 does not refer to the church; it instead points to the time of the Lord's second coming when we shall reign in the millennial kingdom.

Now some may conclude that even though Christians need not keep the ceremonial law they perhaps must still keep the moral law. After a person is saved through faith, he has the power to do good and to keep the law that he may be sanctified. However, we ought to know that as keeping the law is not a condition for salvation, so also keeping the law is not the principle or rule of our Christian life.

"I say unto you, that except your righteousness shall exceed the righteousness of the scribes and Pharisees, ye shall in no wise enter into the kingdom of heaven" (Matt. 5.20). A Pharisee obtains his righteousness by keeping the moral law. Can a Christian enter the kingdom of heaven by having the righteousness of a Pharisee? The Lord emphatically says, No. In this passage (vv.17–20), the Lord twice says "I say unto you". In verse 18 He tells the disciples that the law shall not pass away till all things in it are accomplished. In verse 20 He indicates to them that there needs to be a filling up of what is lacking in the law. Verse 17 tells us that, negatively, the law is not to be destroyed but, positively, to be fulfilled. Thereafter, verses 18 and 19 show us how the Lord's attitude toward law is, negatively, not to destroy it; whereas verse 20 tells us how His attitude toward law is, positively, to fill it full. Because of these two sides, He uses the phrase "I say unto you" twice.

"Your righteousness" in verse 20 is different from being justified before the law. To be justified by God is something which He freely gives to us and is received by faith. "Your righteousness" refers to our conduct which is the result of the working of the Holy Spirit in us. If it were a matter of justification it would have been spoken to sinners. But here the words are addressed to the disciples. Consequently, the righteousness here spoken of is not a God-given righteousness but the righteousness of the saints.

However well the scribes and the Pharisees may conduct themselves, the most they have is the righteousness according to the law. But the disciples are not under law and therefore their righteousness must exceed the righteousness according to the law. Their standard ought to be higher than that of the scribes and the Pharisees. No Christian can enter the kingdom of heaven just by keeping the law. He has the teachings of Matthew 5-7. Unless he follows these teachings he will not be able to enter.

Another point which we must clearly understand is this: Every believer has eternal life, but not all believers shall enter the kingdom of heaven. For eternal life is obtained through God's given righteousness, whereas the kingdom of heaven is entered by means of one's own righteousness. Eternal life is obtained by faith and will never be lost; but the kingdom of heaven is prepared for those who overcome. Eternal life is to be possessed at this age; the kingdom of heaven shall be set up at the Lord's second coming. The Gospel according to John mentions nine times about how eternal life is obtained through faith; yet in Matthew 11 it is stated that "the kingdom of heaven suffereth violence, and men of violence take it by force" (v.12). Once one believes, that one has eternal life; but it takes a daily seeking to enter the kingdom of heaven. To have eternal life refers to how God chooses people out of the world; to enter the kingdom of heaven alludes to how God chooses from among those who have eternal life. Eternal life is granted equally to all, but in the kingdom of heaven there are the great and the least. Now that we have been saved, we need to reproduce through the Holy Spirit our own righteousnesses if we expect to reign with Christ at His return. How can we disbelieve the word spoken by the Lord himself?

Question 17

Some Christians tend to make Galatians 3.21 read as follows: "Is the law then against the promises of God? God forbid: for if there had been a law given which could make righteousness, verily life would have been of the law." Is there any error in this rendering? And if so, where is the error?

Answer:

What Galatians 3.21 actually says is this: "Is the law then against the promises of God? God forbid: for if there had been a law given which could make *alive,* verily *righteousness* would have been of the law." The error in the question is to reverse the order of life and righteousness. We must understand what Paul means here. He is saying that the law and the promises of God are not opposed to each other. The Galatians considered the promise as coming after the law, but Paul proves to them that the promise was made before the law. God had promised Abraham first long before He gave the law to Moses. God gave His promise to Abraham 430 years prior to His giving the law.

An error commonly shared by Christians is that God uses grace to save people after He has failed in using law. God has not done anything of the sort. He made His promise to Abraham without regard to what Abraham would do and actually did. The latter received the promise simply by believing. Since the children of Israel did not appreciate the preciousness of grace, they were given the law by God. His intent in giving them the law was to make them realize their sins in violating the law so that they might better appreciate the promise of God. So that, even after God had given the law, He still saves with grace. The law is given for the knowledge of oneself; and after one knows himself, he will treasure grace. When one is hungry, he thinks of eating. If he does not desire to eat, he needs to have his appetite stimulated by taking some medicine. In similar fashion, the law leads us to grace.

What is meant in Galatians 3.21 is that if there had been a law which could give life, then the law would have also given righteousness. Does the law give life first or give righteousness first? Does a Christian get life first or get righteousness first? Paul argues this point throughout the Letter to the Galatians. He points out that if the law could give us life, then it also could give us righteousness. In our salvation we obtain righteousness before we receive life. Why must a person perish? Because he has sinned. Does sinning occur first or does perishing? Obviously, first comes sinning, and then the perishing. So then, how is a person saved? Because of righteousness. Does righteousness come first or life first? Naturally righteousness precedes life. We can prove this by quoting the Scriptures: "Much more shall they that receive the abundance of grace and of the gift of righteousness reign in life through the one, even Jesus Christ" (Rom. 5.17). In this verse we see that righteousness is put before life. Again: "Even so might grace reign through righteousness unto eternal life through Jesus Christ our Lord" (v.21). Here, too, it is first righteousness and then life. And still another verse from Romans: "The spirit is life because of righteousness" (8.10). Once more the order is first righteousness, followed by life.

One thing which we must be clear about is that the reason we do not have life is because we do not have righteousness. Without righteousness we should be punished and should die according to the righteousness of God. Note that the Lord Jesus came not to be *resurrected* for us first but to *die* for us first and *then* to be resurrected. In believing into Him we appropriate to ourselves the righteousness that He has accomplished and which in turn becomes our life. The spirit is life because of righteousness, says Romans 8.10. Because of the death and resurrection of the Lord Jesus on our behalf, we now have life. The Lord Jesus has already died; and according to the righteousness of God, God cannot but forgive our sins because the price is paid and His righteous demand is satisfied. We are therefore saved by the righteousness which Christ has accomplished in His death. What Paul therefore really means is that if I have said that the law could give life, then I would also have had to say that the law could also give righteousness; but I have not so said, because righteousness is not based on the law. Nevertheless, God still saves people according to the principle of the law, for since the law clearly states that whoever is righteous shall live (see Rom. 10.5; cf. Lev. 18.5), grace gives us righteousness first and afterward life. Thus it is proven that the promises of God do not oppose the law.

Question 18

What is meant by "redemption"? From what are we redeemed?

Answer:

The word "redemption" means to buy out—that is, to
redeem back what has been pledged to others.

Yet to say that we are redeemed, we must ask from
whom or what are we being redeemed? According to the
traditional teaching, we are said to be redeemed from the
hand of the devil because we had become his slaves but that
the Lord Jesus shed His blood to buy us out of the devil's
hand. If so, however, would it be true that God had
conceded to the legality of our being under the hand of the
devil? Let us illustrate our questioning of this. Suppose
someone steals something from you and you know who is
the thief, yet you pay a ransom to buy it back. Such a way
of redeeming would tacitly acknowledge the legality of his
having stolen it from you, which is nonsense. By the same
token, then, if we say that the Lord Jesus pays the price of
His blood to redeem us out of the hand of the devil, that
would be tantamount to saying that God admits to the
lawfulness of the fall of man into the devil's hand. Such an
interpretation is no doubt incorrect. It cannot be said that
we are redeemed from the hand of the devil.

Can it be said, then, that we are redeemed from the
hand of God? No, this too is impossible. For in so saying
this, it will in the first place efface the love of God. Do not
forget that it is God who sent the Lord Jesus to this world.
The Bible tells us again and again how God loves us. (By
contrast the whole New Testament only mentions "the love
of Christ" three times. Now of course the Lord Jesus loves us
too and is therefore willing to come and save us according
to God's will.) Due to His loving us, God laid out the plan
of sending His only Son to save us. Hence we should never
misjudge God's nature. But in the second place, in saying
that we are redeemed from God's hand we are forced to ask,

To whom, then, do we belong? For if we are redeemed from *His* hand, how can we still be His?

Can we say we are redeemed from sin? This too must be answered in the negative. For if we are in fact redeemed from sin, who, then, receives the ransom money? Truly the Lord has paid the price, but sin cannot in any way receive the ransom.

There is only one place in the Bible that can solve this problem. Let us take note of a verse in Galatians, which reads: "Christ redeemed us from the curse of the law, having become a curse for us" (3.13a). Accordingly, our conclusion is that we are redeemed from the curse of the law. Because we were sinners before God we came under the curse of the law. Now, though, the Lord Jesus has died for us, and has thus redeemed us from the curse of the law. Let us carefully notice that we are not redeemed from the law, but rather, from the *curse* of the law. For us to be redeemed from the curse of the law means to be redeemed from its consequence. It is therefore not a matter of being delivered from a few articles of the law, but a being liberated from the curse of the law, because the blood of the Lord Jesus has answered its demand which requires punishment for all who sin. This, therefore, is what the Bible says; and only this much will we say. Our saying any less or saying any more would constitute an error.

Question 19

Does Romans 2.12 advocate that without the law (that is, if God does not give him the law) a person will not perish even though he has sinned? Or that, also, if a sinner has never heard the gospel, will his destiny be one of perishing?

Answer:

Perishing and sin are closely related. To perish or not to perish does not base itself on whether or not there is the law. Romans 2 declares that "as many as have sinned without the law shall also perish without the law" (v.12). God has His way of dealing with people who have not received the law or who have never heard the gospel (see Rom. 2.6–16). First, the just God will not do anything unjust. Second, it is not God's duty or *obligation* to save men, because for men to perish through sin is a self-inflicted consequence; and so God would not be unrighteous by His not saving them. Men are saved not because God is obligated to save, but because God gives special grace.

Hence, to answer this question we must pay special attention to, first, the grace of God, and, second, the righteousness of God. The grace of God has caused the Savior to die and to be resurrected for us. Today we are saved by the righteousness of God because the Lord Jesus has already died and God cannot but save us. If the Lord Jesus had not come and died in our stead, God would still not be unrighteous by not saving us. Grace must come first, and then righteousness follows. Yet, although salvation is *prepared* by grace, it nevertheless is *established* in righteousness. God saves a sinner by sending (through His grace) the Lord Jesus to be the Savior of sinners. If in the future there will be people who go into the lake of fire, there will only be groanings of pain but no murmurings and complaints, because the lake of fire is God's most *just* punishment. In the judgment of the great white throne told of in Revelation 20, no one will rise up and complain that God is not just.

Question 20

Since salvation is based on the death of Christ, why are we told in the Bible to believe in the resurrection of Christ and not just to believe in His death?

Answer:

The apostles were witnesses to the resurrection of the Lord Jesus (Acts 1.22). The book of Acts is filled with words testifying to the Lord's resurrection. Death is only a process, but resurrection is the fulfillment. For this reason the Bible always mentions the Lord's resurrection whenever His death is spoken of. The Lord himself repeatedly told the disciples that He would be killed, but He never stopped with merely mentioning death but always went on to add that on the third day He would be raised from the dead. Resurrection is a sequel to death; in resurrection the work in death is accomplished. The Lord Jesus died on the cross for our sins. How do we know that He has accomplished what He died for? How are we to know that God has accepted what He did? We know because He is risen from the dead. Suppose a criminal is condemned to serve a certain term of years in jail. How do we know whether his term is fulfilled? We know when he comes out of jail. Resurrection therefore concludes death. Without death there can be no resurrection. Yet with resurrection death is passed away. "Whereof he hath given assurance unto all men, in that he hath raised him from the dead" (Acts 17.31). The Lord wants us to believe in His resurrection.

Merely believing in the death of the Lord Jesus will not result in salvation. One must believe in His resurrection in order to be saved. "Believe in thy heart that God raised him from the dead, [and] thou shalt be saved" (Rom 10.9).

Resurrection is an act of God: the Jews "killed the Prince of life whom God raised from the dead" (Acts 3.15). What men can see is death. If the Lord had not been raised from the dead, then the people would have looked at Him as merely a man whom they had killed. But God has raised the Lord Jesus from the dead, thus showing all that "it was not possible that he should be holden of" death (Acts 2.24). For "him did God exalt to his right hand to be a Prince and a Saviour, to give repentance to Israel, and remission of sins" (Acts 5.31). "This is he who is ordained of God to be the Judge of the living and the dead . . . Through his name every one that believeth on him shall receive remission of sins" (Acts 10.42,43).

To believe in resurrection is something beyond human ability. Except a person is moved by the Holy Spirit he is not able to believe that the Lord Jesus has been raised from the dead. To say so without any heart conviction is naturally out of the question. For one to truly believe with the heart it requires the work of the Holy Spirit. "By grace have ye been saved through faith; and that not of yourselves, it is the gift of God" (Eph. 2.8). The apostles bore witness to the resurrection of the Lord Jesus in the power of the Holy Spirit. "They were all filled with the Holy Spirit. . . . And with great power gave the apostles their witness of the resurrection of the Lord Jesus" (Acts 4.31,33).

The work of redemption is accomplished through the death of Christ. Our salvation is based on His death. Nevertheless, we must believe in Christ's resurrection as well as in His death.

Question 21

On the cross Christ declared "It is finished", indicating that the work of the cross is most complete. Why is it we cannot be saved if He is not resurrected?

Answer:

When Christ declared on the cross "It is finished", it is redemption that was accomplished, not salvation that was completed. Redemption is accomplished by Christ and is objective to us, but salvation is not completed until we are saved and is therefore something subjective to us. Our union with Christ in its subjective aspect is a being united with His resurrection. And hence, we cannot be saved unless Christ be resurrected.

"The law of the Spirit of life in Christ Jesus made me free from the law of sin and of death" (Rom. 8.2). Let us notice that this verse speaks of a liberation from two laws: the law of sin and the law of death. Christ's death deals with sin; Christ's resurrection deals with death. By His death He takes away sin; by His resurrection He abrogates death. His death only solves the problem of sin, but His resurrection solves the problem of death. We are not only sinners but also dead persons (see Eph. 2.1). In dying on the cross the Lord saves us from the position of a sinner; in being raised from the dead He delivers us from the position as a dead person.

Had the Lord not died on the cross we would still be sinners. If He had died but had not been resurrected, we might not any longer be sinners, yet we would still be dead men. Only resurrection breaks the power of death. His death is to satisfy the law of God, thus meeting the objective need; His resurrection is to give us life, and therefore fulfills the subjective need. We preach half a gospel if we only preach that Christ died for us and not in addition that Christ was raised for us. In reading the book of Acts we can see how much the apostles stressed the resurrection of our Lord.

The Bible mentions the "blood" over 400 times. For blood is to be brought before God for His satisfaction. This, however, happens after resurrection (see Heb. 9.12). We must pay attention to the Lord's death, yet we cannot separate it from resurrection either. It is both death *and* resurrection. Without resurrection there can be no salvation, because God begets us by the resurrection of Jesus Christ from the dead (1 Peter 1.3).

The Bible is full of the truth of resurrection. Not only the New Testament is full of this truth, the Old Testament is full of it too. Abraham offered Isaac because he believed in resurrection. The crossing of the Jordan River by the children of Israel is a type of resurrection. The budding of Aaron's rod typifies it also. "Christ died for our sins according to the scriptures; . . . he hath been raised on the third day according to the scriptures" (1 Cor. 15.3,4). The phrase according to the scriptures refers to the Old Testament and thus indicates that Christ's resurrection as well as His death are according to what the Old Testament has said.

We praise and thank God, because His Son not only died for us but also has been raised from the dead for us. He deals with the law of death as well as with the law of sin. He saves us from a sinner's position and He delivers us from a dead man's place.

Question 22

Why, after 1 Corinthians 15.3 has said that "Christ died for our sins", does verse 17 say that "if Christ hath not been raised, . . . ye are yet in your sins"?

Answer:

Verse 3 speaks of the relationship of Christ's death with sin, while verse 17 speaks of the relationship of His resurrection with sin. Why is the problem of sin solved by Christ's death in verse 3 and by His resurrection in verse 17? Those who preach the gospel today have the tendency to emphasize the death of Christ a great deal but to overlook the resurrection of Christ. Frequently we may hear how Christ's death saves us from sin but seldom do we hear people say His resurrection delivers us from sin.

Christ's death does save us from the penalty of sin and does cancel out our criminal case before God; but to be delivered from the power of sin must depend on Christ's resurrection. As we read the book of Acts, which of the two do the apostles speak of more—death or resurrection? Take also 1 Corinthians 15. Is Paul there trying to prove the death of Christ or the resurrection of Christ? We know the apostles placed their emphasis on His resurrection. The world believes that the Lord Jesus has died, but the world finds it hard to believe that He died for our sins. How do we know that He really died for our sins? This difficult question is solved by His resurrection. His resurrection proves that He has died for the purpose of bearing our sins. Now that the problem of sin is solved, He is raised from the dead. When you tell people that the Lord Jesus died for our sins, they will believe if the Holy Spirit reveals the risen

Christ to them. The resurrection of Christ can alone prove that His death is for bearing our sins.

Christ's resurrection not only proves that His death was for bearing the sins of the world, it also gives us a new life. Christ must die and be raised for us. I am one who has sinned, but the Lord Jesus has died for me and atoned for my sins. Yet can I live before God by my flesh? Can I go back to sin? True, Christ's death has cleared my old debts, but His death does not guarantee my not incurring new debts. Christ must be resurrected and a new life must be put in me that I may live a life different from the former one. Death clears my sinful case; resurrection makes me sin no more. Consequently, the Lord Jesus not only has died and atoned for our sins before God but He also is resurrected to live within us, to bear our problems, and to enable us to overcome temptations and sins. If He is not raised from the dead, we still will lack the power not to contract new debts even though our old debts are all paid. This explains why Christ must be raised from the dead so as to solve our future problem. We must believe that the Lord Jesus is risen and dwells in us as well as believe that He bore our sins in His death. We are regenerated through the resurrection of the Lord Jesus (1 Peter 1.3). God has put a new life in us, and this life is resurrection life—a life that knows no bounds—so that we may live as Christ lives.

Many people entertain a basic error in their thinking: they only accept the death work of the Lord Jesus without accepting also His resurrection work. Some Christians often complain how adverse are their circumstances and how difficult are their families. They cannot overcome because their temptations are simply too real. We tend to forget that just as the temptations are real, so the Christ who indwells us is equally real. God puts us in a difficult situation for two reasons: one is to prove to us how very real is the Christ who

indwells us, and the other is to cause us to declare with
satisfaction that the indwelling Christ is truly most real. We
are to overcome sin by the indwelling Christ not just once
or twice or three times, but many many times. Many of
God's people pay attention to the Savior who lives outside
them and forget the same Savior who lives within them.
They look to the Savior at Calvary but overlook the same
Savior inside them. Due to the reality of *this* life in us, we
may overcome every and all temptation.

We should now be clear that death solves the problem
of sin whereas resurrection gives us a new life that we may
not sin.

Question 23

Why does the Bible call upon us to believe in the Son of
God? What is meant by believing in the Son of God? To
believe in the Son of God answers to which part of the
many works that Christ has done for us? If a person only
believes in the Son of Man, will he nevertheless be saved?

Answer:

Because Christ is lifted up in the capacity of the Son of
Man (John 8.28), He includes all mankind in Him. Since
Christ died for all, therefore all died (2 Cor. 5.14). Even as
the action of the one man Adam involved all mankind in
Adam, so the work of the one man Christ embraces all
mankind in Christ too. We must see how Christ includes all
mankind before we can understand what redemption is.

Hebrews 7.4–10 shows us that the priestly ministry of

Melchizedek is greater than that of the Levites because Melchizedek received a tithe from Abraham and also that he blessed Abraham. Melchizedek was therefore greater than the Levites. But why was this so? It is because Levi "was yet in the loins of his father, when Melchizedek met him" (v.10). We know that Abraham begat Isaac, Isaac Jacob, and Jacob Levi—which made Levi the great grandson of Abraham. When Abraham offered the tithe and received the blessing, not only was Levi not yet born, even Levi's father and grandfather had not yet been born. But the Bible reckons the offering of the tithe and the receiving of a blessing by Abraham as constituting the offering of the tithe and the receiving of a blessing by Levi. Since Abraham was less than Melchizedek, naturally Levi too was less than Melchizedek. All this is to show us that when Adam sinned, all mankind was in Adam as well; therefore, all have sinned. And in like manner, when Christ died, all were in Him, and hence all have died.

Christ as the Son of Man is the conclusion of all who descend from Adam; but Christ as the Son of God commences a new creation. Christ is the last Adam, and by His death He concludes the old creation. But by His resurrection Christ commences a new creation. By His death He deals with sin; by His resurrection He gives us life. Consequently, the Bible calls upon us to believe in the Son of God.

To believe in the Son of God means to believe in the Lord's resurrection. For the Lord "was declared to be the Son of God with power, according to the spirit of holiness, by the resurrection from the dead" (Rom. 1.4). Moreover, Psalm 2 reads: "Thou art my son; this day have I begotten thee" (v.7). And Acts 13.33 tells us that the resurrection of the Lord Jesus is the fulfillment of this word in Psalm 2.7.

Believing in the Son of God is related to the resurrection which Christ has accomplished for us.

No one can be saved by only believing in Christ as the Son of Man and not also as the Son of God. One must believe in Him as both the Son of Man and the Son of God in order to be saved. For He has not only died but also been resurrected. He not only has borne our sins but also abolished death. He gives us eternal life as well as saves us from perishing.

Question 24

What is the most important miracle in the Old Testament? To what does this miracle point?

Answer:

The most important miracle in the Old Testament is that concerning Jonah, and this miracle points to the resurrection of the Lord Jesus from the dead.

Some people apply a wrong emphasis to this miracle. They consider Jonah's being in the belly of the fish for three days and three nights as a miracle which typifies the three days and three nights which our Lord spent in the heart of the earth. Let it be known that to be buried for three days and three nights in the earth after death is not a miracle, inasmuch as burial after death is quite the common occurrence. For a person to jump into the sea and to be swallowed by a big fish is also not beyond the realm of possibility. Not only is it not a miracle to be in the belly of a fish for three days and three nights, even to be there for *fifty* days and *fifty* nights is no miracle either. What *is* miraculous is to *come out* of the belly of a fish after three days and three nights. For Christ to be in the grave three days and three nights is nothing extraordinary, but for Him to be raised from the tomb after three days and three nights, that *is* extraordinary and hence a miracle. Death is therefore not a miracle; but resurrection *is* a miracle.

Jonah had made up his own mind; and he would not turn back toward Nineveh until he had suffered, so full was he of racial prejudice. God had ordered him to go to Nineveh but he chose to go to Tarshish. He had therefore disobeyed God, and God would not let him go free. So God raised up such a storm in the sea that the boat was likely to be broken. Jonah at last realized in his heart that he was the cause of this disaster. Finally he was forced to ask the mariners to cast him into the sea, whereupon the storm subsided. God then ordered a big fish to swallow him, and Jonah remained in its belly for three days and three nights. Afterward God spoke to the fish, and it vomited Jonah upon the dry land. Only then did Jonah obey the command of God to go to Nineveh and preach the gospel. If you look for inward peace, therefore, this old man of yours—even this Jonah—must be cast into the sea.

Jonah was a person who rebelled and fled from the will of God. He was thrown into the sea because of his own sin. Not so though with out Lord, for He was crucified on behalf of the sins of others. After Jonah was tossed into the sea, the storm subsided. But it is also true that once the Lord Jesus has died, men are reconciled to God. Whenever we accept the position given us by the Lord Jesus, we obtain peace. Jonah must be cast into the sea; our Lord Jesus must die. And we too must die, that is, be made a partaker of His death.

Jonah's being thrown into the sea and swallowed and taken into the belly of the fish typifies burial. The one and only meaning of burial is this: that we may not see the dead. After his wife Sarah died, Abraham spoke to the children of Heth, saying, "Give me a possession of a buryingplace with you, that I may bury my dead out of my sight" (Gen. 23.4). In baptism we acknowledge that the death of the Lord Jesus is real and our having died with Him is also real. We have died with Him, and thus we have also been buried with Him. On the other hand, Jonah's being vomited by the fish onto dry land typifies resurrection. The Lord Jesus has been raised from the grave; but we too have been raised with Him.

The resurrection of the Lord Jesus is the heart of all miracles. Resurrection is more than an objective fact, it also is a subjective experience. Before Jonah was cast into the sea, he would rather have died than go to Nineveh; but after he was vomited by the fish onto dry land, he went without resistance to Nineveh. The basic change wrought in him was due to the work of resurrection. After you are saved and experience resurrection, you will be willing to do what before you would rather have died first than do. Formerly you suffered defeats in many things and simply could not overcome; but now, after you have received His resurrection life, you undergo a drastic change.

Question 25

Adam is created by God, not born of God; Christ is begotten of God, not created by God. Are we Christians born of God or created by God?

Answer:

Some people profess to believe the whole Bible, yet they do not believe in the regeneration of a Christian. They even maintain that regeneration belongs to the Jews, for Christians are newly created, not regenerated. However, the Bible teaches that Christians are born of God as well as being God's new creation: "That which is born of the flesh is flesh; and that which is born of the Spirit is spirit" (John 3.6); "Begat us again . . . by the resurrection of Jesus Christ from the dead" (1 Peter 1.3). We are reminded from the Scriptures that as there is a begetting of the flesh so there is a begetting of the Spirit. "If any man is in Christ, he is a new creature: the old things are passed away; behold, they are become new" (2 Cor. 5.17). In mentioning regeneration the Bible reminds us of how we once had an Adamic life; in mentioning the new creation the Bible enjoins us not to think of the old but to think of Christ.

We are newly created in Christ. This not only speaks of position but also includes experience. Position and experience are different, but they cannot be separated. According to position the Corinthian believers are already sanctified and justified; but according to experience their lives are marked by jealousy and strife. We may differentiate these two matters in this way, yet to completely separate them tends to make us forget the accomplished work of Christ and to focus on our own experience. The more we look into our own experience the less experience we will have. If our eyes turn to Christ we will be transformed into His image. We must not look at ourselves but look to Christ alone, and then shall we have real experience.

What is meant by living in ourselves? It means turning constantly to think of ourselves. By turning to think of ourselves we immediately begin to live in ourselves. Humility, however, is not a thinking of oneself; and it is not just a thinking less of oneself, since thinking less is still a thinking of oneself. Our union with Christ is more than a union of position, it is also a union of life (so, for that matter, was our being in Adam). All who looked at the brazen serpent received the healing effect on them (see Num. 21.9). Hence looking away from ourselves to Christ alone gives us the victory.

Question 26

What is meant by "being now justified by his blood" (Rom. 5.9)? And what is meant by "raised for our justification" (Rom. 4.25)?

Answer:

How are we going to connect "being now justified by his blood" (Rom. 5.9) and "raised for our justification" (Rom. 4.25)? Let us first examine what is meant by "justified by his blood" and by "raised for our justification", and how wide is the scope of justification by blood and the scope of justification by resurrection.

Justification, according to the Bible, has two meanings: (1) that you have no sin, and (2) that God looks upon you as being righteous, as being perfect. Before they sinned, Adam and Eve were not sinners, yet they were not justified by God either. Christ, though, is righteous and most perfect in the sight of God. To every Christian who comes before Him God will tell him not only that he is a sinner forgiven but also that he is righteous. He not only does not have any defilement of sin, he also is clothed with the robe of righteousness. Everyone who comes to God in Christ is accepted by God even as Christ is accepted.

What is the difference between justification by blood and justification by resurrection? Our criminal case before God is resolved by the blood of the Lord Jesus, because He has shed His blood to annul our case. But we are accepted by God through the resurrection of the Lord Jesus. Many Christians share a common error of thinking, which is, that they assume the forgiveness of sins to be everything. Yes indeed, we should rejoice for the forgiveness of sins; nonetheless, what God gives to us in Christ is more than just forgiveness. We ought to know that forgiveness is not the whole of salvation. Some have expressed the thought that if they can only so much as climb into heaven they will be satisfied, while others believe that if they can barely stand within the threshold of heaven they shall be content. Should we think in this manner, we betray our great ignorance as to what the grace of God is.

The Scriptures tell us that the grace of God has obtained for us not only the forgiveness of our sins but also a most glorious position, which is, that as we come before God we are accepted in His eyes: "to the praise of the glory of his grace, wherein he has taken us into favour [or acceptance] in the Beloved" (Eph. 1.6 Darby). We are accepted as well as forgiven. The dying thief on the cross is accepted just as much by God as are the apostles John, Peter, and Paul. In the eyes of God, the one who is in Christ is spotless as well as blameless. What is being spotless? Let us suppose that my hand is cut. After the cut is healed there still remains a scar. Though danger no longer exists today, the scar yet proves that once there had been an accident. But the Bible tells us that God is able to save us to the point of spotlessness. That is, God can save us to the point where we will no longer recall our past sinful life nor feel any uneasiness. The work of God is always so perfect. He not only forgives our sins but also makes us righteous.

The blood atones for our sins before God, and this is the objective side. The blood also cleanses the conscience (Heb. 9.14). Each time you think of sin you remember how the blood has cleansed you of your sins, and your heart is peaceful. This is the subjective effect of the blood. The Lord Jesus has shed His blood to atone for our sins before God, thus solving the problem of sin. At the same time His blood cleanses our conscience. What is conscience? Whenever we sin there is always within us that word which points out our sin and makes us uneasy. The blood of the Lord can cleanse our conscience so as to make it void of offense (Acts 24.16). If a Christian is always experiencing an accusation in his conscience, this does not indicate humility on his part; it instead indicates an unbelief in God's word and a despising of the work of Christ. Our conscience should not be under constant accusation for our past sins; we should believe that the blood has washed them all away.

There was once a woman who was already more than fifty years old. Over twenty years ago, she committed a most disgraceful sin and continued in that sin for several months. Though she had long repented, there was always an accusing voice which said that the sin she had committed was unpardonable. She accordingly had no peace. Then she met a preacher to whom she revealed her history and also her grief and restlessness. Whereupon the preacher asked her if she had ever read 1 John 1.7. She said she did. The preacher then suggested that they read together the last clause of that verse—"and the blood of Jesus his Son cleanseth us from all sin"—and then asked, "Now aside from that particular sin, have you committed any other sins?" "Indeed, I *have* committed other sins, but all those others have been cleansed by the blood, whereas this sin remains uncleansed," answered the woman. "But *my* Bible says, 'cleanseth us from *all* sin', not 'cleanseth us from *other* sins'," the preacher continued.

He also asked her to read verse 9 with him—"If we confess our sins, he is faithful and righteous to forgive us our sins, and to cleanse us from all unrighteousness"—and after finishing reading it he asked her, "How would the faithful and righteous God forgive and cleanse you?" "By confessing my sins," replied the woman. "Have you confessed?" "I *have* confessed, hundreds of times." "Well, God says that if you confess your sin, He will forgive and cleanse. You have confessed, and He has already forgiven and cleansed you." "But I do not feel it," responded the woman. "Does it really matter how you feel, if God in heaven has forgiven and cleansed you?" "No, it really does not matter," she replied.

Later they prayed together. But before they prayed, the preacher told her, "Prayer is effective only if you believe what the Bible says; prayer is useless if you do not believe." In simple words he committed her to God, asking Him to make her believe that her sin had been forgiven and cleansed. Then she prayed, saying, "O God, my former fault was not believing in the work of Christ. Now I do believe in His work, I believe Your word. Therefore, earlier my sin *had* been forgiven and cleansed." Someone met this sister afterward and asked her how she was. She quickly answered, "Fine, very fine!"

Many people are not clear on this point; consequently, they daily see their sins and not the sinner's Savior, their sins but not God's grace, their sins yet not Christ's work. The irony of it all is this: that whoever thinks more of his own sin, sins the more. If one looks to the Lord Jesus and believes in His finished work, he will soon forget his particular sin. We are saved by looking to the Lord, not by recollecting about ourselves. The more anyone gives attention to one particular sin the harder will it be to be rid of that sin. But if he should look to the Lord he will be transformed from glory to glory according to the Lord's image (see 2 Cor. 3.18).

We are justified by resurrection. And this is the positive aspect. In being raised from the dead He imparts the new life to us. This life in us is as righteous as the Lord is righteous: it cannot sin; so that when God sees this life in us He reckons us as righteous. Christ's resurrection does not only give us new life, it also causes our life to be hid with Christ in God (Col. 3.3). Subjectively speaking, Christ is our life; He dwells in us. The life which we obtain at the time of regeneration is a resurrection life. Objectively speaking, however, we appear before God in Christ. We have a new position, which causes God to look upon us as though looking upon Christ. Hence we need not tremble with fear when we approach God; instead, we may say, Hallelujah! We may draw nigh to God with boldness and fullness of faith. We may say to Him, You are our Father and we are Your children. Who then can condemn us, for we have God justifying us? As we appear before Him in Christ, there is nothing more beautiful than this. In a hymn written by Catesby Paget, there are these words:

> So nigh, so very nigh to God,
>   I cannot nearer be;
> For in the person of His Son
>   I am as near as He.
>
> So dear, so very dear to God,
>   More dear I cannot be;
> The love wherewith He loves the Son,
>   Such is His love to me.

The life within us is Christ-given, but so too is our position before God given by Christ. The reason many Christians do not grow properly is because their conscience is under accusation and so they have no liberty before God. When there is a hole in the conscience, faith soon leaks out. If our conscience is accused, our faith in prayer becomes greatly weakened.

Being justified by the blood our problem regarding sin is solved; God will look upon us as though we have no sin. Being justified by resurrection we have Christ in us as our life, and this gives us a new position before God—a relationship with God such as that between Christ and God.

Question 27

There are two sides to the crucifixion of Christ—His being crucified by men and His being crucified by God. The verses in Acts 2.23,36 and 3.15 speak of *men* crucifying Him, while those in Is. 53.6,10 speak of *God* crucifying Him. Which part of His crucifixion is done by men and which part is done by God?

Answer:

In studying the Scriptures we can clearly see that the crucifixion of Christ has both the men-crucifying-Him aspect and the God-crucifying-Him aspect. Judging by the seven words the Lord spoke from the cross, we may know which part of His crucifixion was done by men and which part by God. According to our human estimate, His crucifixion lasts for six hours. During the first three hours He spoke three words; during the last three hours He

uttered four words. Why did He not say more or less during
the first three hours? After a careful study we will know that
the first three hours of His crucifixion is the period of men's
work, whereas the last three hours is the period of God's
work.

The first three hours lasted from nine in the morning
until noon (Mark 15.25), when the Lord was crucified,
mocked, railed at, and reproached by men. All His
sufferings were heaped upon Him by men.

But the last three hours, which extended from noon to
three o'clock in the afternoon, were when Christ suffered at
the hands of God. For during these three hours darkness
covered the whole land, distinctly not an act of men. The
veil in the temple was suddenly rent into two from top to
bottom; this also was beyond human capability. The earth
quaked, the rocks were rent, and the tombs were opened;
obviously none of these was men's work. These were all
done by God.

During the first part of Christ's crucifixion, men did
everything they could do to Him; in the second part of His
crucifixion, God also did all that He could possibly do. The
first part of the cross expressed all the hatred of men toward
God; the second part of the cross reveals all the love of God
toward men. Hence the cross, as some people would say,
became the meeting point of love and hate.

Let us first look at the three words spoken during the
initial three hours.

The opening word was: "Father, forgive them; for they
know not what they do" (Luke 23.34). How could God
forgive those who murdered an innocent person? How
could the Lord pray in this way? If God should answer this
prayer will He not be guilty of being unrighteous? In
answering these questions we need to recognize clearly that
the Lord Jesus was crucified to bear the sin of the world.

The righteous God could only forgive our sins at the cross, because "apart from shedding of blood there is no remission" (Heb. 9.22). And the Lord Jesus could pray such a prayer only on the ground of the cross. Otherwise, God's forgiveness as well as the Lord's prayer would both be unrighteous.

The second word was: "He said unto him, Verily I say unto thee, today shalt thou be with me in Paradise" (Luke 23.43). How could a malefactor enter Paradise? For were all malefactors permitted to enter Paradise would it be any longer a garden of pleasure? Yet all these considerations are human reasonings. In the eyes of God, not only the malefactors cannot enter Paradise, even the so-called "good people" are not able to enter there. For all in Adam have sinned (Rom. 5.12). The Lord Jesus was able to say such a word to the repentant malefactor because He is the one mediator between God and men (1 Tim. 2.5) as well as the Lamb of God (John 1.29). Through the eternal Spirit He offered himself without blemish to God in order that His blood might cleanse our conscience from dead works (Heb. 9.14). That malefactor in Paradise is no longer a malefactor, but one whose conscience has been cleansed from dead works. All who receive the Lord—that is, who believe in His name—have the same experience.

The third word: "He saith unto his mother, Woman, behold, thy son! Then saith he to the disciple, Behold, thy mother!" (John 19.26,27) Here we are shown that due to what the Lord has done on the cross we now have a new relationship with God and with men; we are now fellow-citizens with the saints and of the household of God. We may have fellowship not only with God but also with one another. Not just John at that time could receive Mary as his mother according to the word of the Lord, even Paul (see Rom. 16.13) and all the rest of the saints throughout the ages can have the same feeling. How marvelous this is! Sharing the same life gives all the saints a new relationship.

After the Lord Jesus finished uttering these three words the earth was covered with darkness. God had heard the prayer offered by the Lord and had put all the sins of the world upon Him. God had made Him who knew no sin to be sin on our behalf. God therefore now saves us not only on the ground of His grace but also on the ground of His righteousness. He has bestowed mercy on us, but He has also given One who has paid the price for us all, who has repaid every penny we ever owed.

And so around three o'clock in the afternoon, the Lord began to utter four more words.

The fourth word was this: "My God, my God, why hast thou forsaken me?" (Matt. 27.46) Many martyrs who have been under persecution and severe punishments have felt the nearness of God to them and have borne their sufferings with dignity. Yet how much closer God would have been to our Lord (whose whole life had been spent in obedience to God) if He had merely been crucified through the persecution that came from men! How could God ever forsake Him when men forsook Him? Praise and thanks be to God, on the cross our Lord did not die a martyr's death; rather, He died in bearing the sins of all mankind: for God put our sins on Him: it was God himself who crucified the Lord. After the Lord had spoken the first three words, He knew that God had heard His prayer and had put the sins of all mankind upon Him; and consequently, He also knew that God had now forsaken Him.

The fifth word simply came as: "I thirst" (John 19.28). Thirstiness is a condition in hell; thirstiness is the characteristic of the sufferings of hell. The rich man in Luke 16 was in the fire of Hades without even a drop of water to cool his tongue. There is no place more thirsty than hell. At this particular moment the Lord suffered the penalty of hell on men's behalf and tasted death for every man (Heb. 2.9).

The sixth word was: "It is finished" (John 19.30). This indicates that the work of redemption is finished, for the Lord by this time has borne the sin of the world and received sin's penalty for the world.

And finally, *the seventh word:* "Father, into thy hands I commit my spirit" (Luke 23.46 Darby). Some time earlier the Lord had cried out, "My God, my God, why hast thou forsaken me?" This was because He stood on the ground of bearing our sins. But now He utters the word "Father" to indicate that the work of redemption has been accomplished and that His fellowship with the Father is now instantly restored. The Lord laid down His life voluntarily, and He committed His life to God: "No one taketh it away from me, but I lay it down of myself. I have power to lay it down, and I have power to take it again" (John 10.18). If this were not the case, then not even a hundred crosses could have taken our Lord's life away.

Our sins are thus taken away by the most righteous Lord. According to His righteousness God must forgive us, because Christ has already died and become a sin-offering.

Yet some people may ask, Since the Lord accomplishes the work of redemption by His death on the cross, how could He have forgiven people's sins *before* His death? This is because, even before Christ died, God has already reckoned the cross as an accomplished fact: "Whosoever believeth on him should not perish, but have eternal life" (John 3.16); "He that eateth my flesh and drinketh my blood hath eternal life" (6.54). These passages show us that even when the Lord was on earth all who believed in Him would have eternal life. Moreover, we read in Revelation about "the Lamb that hath been slain from the foundation of the world" (13.8 mg.; cf. also 1 Peter 1.19,20). The Lord is indeed the Lamb that has been slain from before the foundation of the world. Consequently, the church is not limited by space (for the body of Christ is one), and the cross is not restricted by time. (For even in the Old Testament period God could forgive people. Under the Old Covenant—see Numbers 35.25–28—if any person should kill another accidentally he could flee to a city of refuge, where no one could seize his life and where he would become free once the high priest had died. This is a type of the fact that even before Christ's death, if anyone should hide himself in Christ, he was safe and would become free upon the death of Christ who is *the* high priest of God.)

Question 28

John 19.30 says "It is finished" whereas Colossians has Paul saying: "I . . . fill up on my part that which is lacking of the afflictions of Christ" (1.24). What is finished and what is still lacking?

Answer:

At first glance these two passages may appear to be contradictory; but with careful reading, the distinctiveness of each can be seen.

"It is finished" points to the propitiation of the Lord Jesus. It refers to the penalty which the Lord took on the cross; it speaks of the sufferings for sins which He received from God's hand.

"Afflictions" is sometimes translated as "tribulations" or "distresses". The "afflictions" here noted refer to the afflictions which come from human hands. What afflictions Christ received from God's hand none else could share; all were solely fulfilled in the Lord. But at the same time there is still a lack in those afflictions of Christ which He suffered from human hands. And this is the part which every Christian is called upon to share in and to fill up.

The work of redemption has been accomplished. Unfortunately, however, many Christians do not seem to clearly comprehend it. Some are still thinking that if their conduct is good they will somehow be more fit to go to heaven and will thus have more confidence in entering in; but that if they do not behave themselves they will not dare enter heaven boldly, but instead will feel like crawling into heaven. Nothing could be further from fact. Suppose the malefactor who was crucified with Christ had lived on after he believed in the Lord. Suppose he had come down from the cross and had lived for several decades more. Let us suppose further that during these years his work was ten times more than that of Paul's, his love grew ten times more than that of John's, and that he saved ten times more people than did Peter. Would it make any difference if he went to heaven then or on the day he was crucified? Would it make him worthier after all those years? All who know the grace of God realize that he was not one bit worthier afterward than on the first day. Why? Because the qualification for entry into heaven is entirely founded upon the Lord and His work. None who believes is ever unfit for heaven, nor is anyone ever more worthy to enter heaven. The work of redemption has been accomplished by Christ, and no one can add anything to it. Even if one should become what is commonly acknowledged by the world as a sage, his qualification for heaven is still founded upon the "It is finished" of Christ.

Yet let us not misconstrue this as permitting believers to

sin. Far be the thought. If a saved believer does not behave, he will not be able to enter the kingdom, even though he is not thereby barred from heaven. Whatever may be our conduct, it does not alter our entry into heaven. Even God cannot change the situation, because as the Lord Jesus was crucified I was judged and am therefore dead. How, then, can God ever be unrighteous? Since he has already accepted Christ's death as my death, He will no longer judge and condemn me. It is finished; and, it is unchangeable. Nevertheless, if we continue to sin we will be placed outside the kingdom—that is, outside the glory of the kingdom.

There are two places in Romans which refer especially to the glory of God. One is: "All have sinned, and fall short of the glory of God" (Rom. 3.23); the other is: "Through whom also we have had our access by faith into this grace wherein we stand; and we rejoice in hope of the glory of God" (Rom. 5.2). Falling short of the glory of God is due to sins; rejoicing in hope of the glory of God is due to the blood. Whatever loss sin has incurred the blood has not only replenished but added on much more. Because of the death of Christ we may rejoice in hope of the glory of God.

The redemptive work of Christ is finished, but the afflictions of Christ remain to be filled up. He has already accomplished redemption; yet do all people know what He has done? Probably many do not know. For this reason we must go and tell the world what Christ has accomplished. Christ himself only preached the gospel to those who had direct contact with Him and therefore He was limited to the people of His generation. His afflictions among men are still lacking; consequently, we today must take up the responsibility to preach the gospel. In preaching the gospel, afflictions are unavoidable. To preach the gospel may appear foolish to the world; to distribute a tract may cause blushing on the face. Nevertheless, these afflictions and more are what we must take. For what Christ has accomplished is only the work of redemption; there is still a lacking in the tribulations, the distresses, and the afflictions involved in the spreading of the news of this redemptive work. Hence we must go and spread it.

Question 29

What is the difference between "Christ died for us" (Rom. 5.8) and "Christ died for our sins" (1 Cor. 15.3)?

Answer:

"Christ died for us" means that Christ died for us sinners. The purpose of His death is to save us sinners. What He has accomplished is for us; that is, to gain us, and to deliver us from ourselves.

"Christ died for our sins" signifies that He died for the sins committed by us sinners. The purpose is to take away our sins so that they may be forgiven, and to save us from the penalty and the power of sin so that we are no longer under its dominion.

Question 30

In God's plan of redemption do Christians change position with Christ? In other words, does He who is righteous become unrighteous but that we who are unrighteous become righteous? (2 Cor. 5.21)

Answer:

In God's plan of redemption the Christian and Christ do not exchange places, but there *is* a union involved: "Him who knew no sin he [God] made to be sin on our behalf; that we might become the righteousness of God in him" (2 Cor. 5.21).

Nowhere in the Scriptures are we told that Christians and Christ have exchanged positions. Why is it, then, that we often say: I am saved because though I have sinned Christ died for me? We need to understand that such a way of speaking refers exclusively to our personal welfare. The question that is asked here, however, is concerned with the matter of position in God's plan of redemption. From the viewpoint of our personal gain it is true that Christ died for us; but in God's redemptive plan, if I were to say that Christ stood in my sinner's place and died for me—that would make God unrighteous. For how can God condemn Christ as being unrighteous, knowing full well that Christ is righteous? But then, too, how can God justify me whom He knows to be a sinner? Hence in God's plan of redemption the Christian and Christ do not exchange positions but instead come into a union.

Let us again read 2 Corinthians 5.21: "Him who knew no sin he made to be sin on our behalf"; God made the One who had never sinned, and who knew not what sin was, to be sin for us. The phrase "to be sin" does not signify merely to bear or to carry our sins. Because if it is only bearing, there is always the possibility of not bearing: if it is only carrying, it is merely a being carried in the body. Yet on the cross Christ not only bore or carried our sins, He was made to be sin for us. The Lord Jesus was united with us to such an extent that He was made to be sin as well as to bear and carry our sins. So when God judged Him, He judged sin; when God punished Him, He punished sin.

There are three things we ought to know about God's plan of redemption, and three phrases can best summarize them: the first is "God and me", the second is "God for me", and the third is "God in me". "God and me" lays the foundation for the success of God's plan of redemption. "God for me" accomplishes God's redemption for me. And "God in me" works in me what God has accomplished. For in the Word becoming flesh, God and man are joined into one in the Lord Jesus. This is "God and me". Because the Lord is both God and man He can die and be resurrected for us, thus becoming the mighty Savior. In order for God to dwell in me, He must send from heaven His Holy Spirit. When the Lord was on earth He was clothed with flesh; but in dwelling in us today He is clothed with the Spirit. Hence some say that the Holy Spirit is the second Self of the Lord Jesus Christ. The Holy Spirit comes to work in us, to accomplish in us all which God has already accomplished in Christ. If there is no "God and me", there can never be "God for me" nor "God in me". Had the Lord Jesus not been born to become a man He could never die. In dying on the cross He did not bear the sin of the world in the capacity of a third person. No, He became sin for us and died for us in the capacity of a man.

On the one hand, it is indeed true that God has put all our sins on the Lord and thus the Lord has borne our sins. On the other hand, in God's plan of redemption He has judged the Lord Jesus and in so doing has judged us and judged sin. We can therefore thank God today for the fact that the Lord has become sin for us on the cross.

What is the consequence of Christ being made sin on our behalf? that we may become righteous? that we may be righteous in Him? Not this, but "that we might become the righteousness of God in him", as is indicated in our verse. We should not only notice the words "in him" but also pay attention to the words "the righteousness of God". In being made sin for us, Christ does not change us to be righteous nor make us no more sinners; rather, He causes us to become the righteousness of God in himself. Every saved Christian becomes the righteousness of God. It is the righteousness of God which saves us. It is God who has made Christ to be sin for us. In judging the Lord Jesus, God has judged us as well as judged sin. He reckons us as righteous, yet not because we ourselves are righteous; this is a purely objective matter.

People may, according to their view, say to us that we are not very good. The fact is, however, that we are not made to be righteous in Christ but we become the righteousness of God in Christ, thus proving that it is the righteousness of God which so saves us. If we are clear on this point our problems will be greatly lessened in our daily life. For the Lord to be on the cross is for Him to be reckoned as sin on the cross. There God has condemned sin and solved the problem of sin. And so we are free.

Question 31

When is our union with Christ—both objectively and subjectively—actualized?

Answer:

Considering the objective side, we may say that our union with Christ is actualized at the time of His death on the cross. "One died for all, therefore all died" (2 Cor. 5.14). When Christ died He took all the people of the world to the cross with Him, and therefore all died in Him.

Judging the subjective side, our union with Christ is actualized at the time we are born again, that is, by virtue of the Lord's resurrection. By reading Romans 6.3-5, and also Chapter 8, we may clearly see this fact. Our union with Christ on the subjective side is effected in His resurrection. What does baptism represent? It represents death. Viewed objectively, when we are baptized we are saying that we have already died, because only the dead are buried. We are acknowledging that the death is real, and so we accept the burial. But resurrection comes after the burial: a rising after being buried is resurrection. In our daily life we are not seeking death, since we confess that we have already died in Christ; instead, we are daily allowing the resurrection life to be lived out through us. Romans 6 requires us to do one thing, which is to yield (or to consecrate). The minds and hearts of many people are bent on experiencing death, but they are unable to put themselves to death. We should realize that after we believe in the Lord the first thing for us to do is to be buried, not to die. We are to acknowledge our death, not to beg for our death.

There is another point to be raised in this discussion. Suppose people talk about the cross by stating that first, the Lord died on the cross for me; second, the Lord died on the cross as me; and third, the Lord died on the cross with me. Is such a statement scriptural? Laying aside the first two points, let us focus on the third. Is there any error in saying "the Lord died on the cross with me"? In searching the

New Testament, nowhere can we find such a statement that Christ died with me. The Bible says instead, "I have been crucified with Christ" (Gal. 2.20). It also says in Galatians 6.14 that through the cross of the Lord Jesus Christ you and I have been crucified to the world. Simply by reading these two passages we ought to know that *we* have died with *Christ,* not that Christ died with us. This is because our union with His death is an objective fact. Christ died once, and forever. We have already died in His death.

To say that He died with us would be to turn that which is objective into that which is subjective; and it would mean that Christ must be offered up many times: today Christ must die with Mr. Chang, and tomorrow with Mr. Yu. If a thousand persons believe in Him, He would need to die afresh a thousand times. Let us remember this well, that the Scriptures only tell us this truth—that "we have died with Christ" and not that "Christ died with us". Do not think that reversing the order is of no importance, because in fact such inversion unsettles the truth. The word of the Lord allows no inversion.

Question 32

Why does the Bible say we are "in the Lord", "in Christ", or "in Christ Jesus", but never "in Jesus" or "in Jesus Christ"?

Answer:

Let us be aware first of all that the passage in 1 Thessalonians 4.14 rendered "even so them also that are fallen asleep in Jesus" should be translated as "them that are fallen asleep *through* Jesus" (ASV mg.). In no other place in the Bible can such a phrase as "in Jesus" or "in Jesus Christ" be found in connection with our relationship to Christ. The Scriptures always say "in the Lord" or "in Christ" or "in Christ Jesus". For these phrases convey something of tremendous significance toward us as well as toward atonement.

"Jesus" is the name given Him at His birth. It is His lowly name as a man. "Christ" (which means, the Anointed) is the name given Him when He is anointed by God after His resurrection (see Acts 2.36). It is His glorious name.

"Jesus Christ" conveys the thought that this lowly Jesus is to be Christ in the future; while "Christ Jesus" means that the Christ who is now is the same who was Jesus before.

Why not "in Jesus" or "in Jesus Christ"? This is because we are not united to the Lord while He lived on earth. We have no union with Him on His Son of Man side. "Jesus" is His name as the Son of Man. He as the Son of Man is far above all men in virtue and in beauty. With such a life we have no portion. The meaning of "Jesus" is Savior. We are not united with Jesus because we do not, together with Him, save people.

To say "in the Lord", "in Christ", or "in Christ Jesus" is to indicate that due to Christ's being raised from the dead, God has made Him both Lord and Christ, and in that respect we do have a share in Him, because we have a share in His resurrection. God has put us in His resurrection. Our subjective experience is actualized in His resurrection.

"Jesus" is a personal name, whereas "Christ" is a name corporate as well as personal: "As the body is one, and hath many members, and all the members of the body, being many, are one body; so also is Christ" (1 Cor. 12.12). Here it does not say "so also is Christ and the church"; it simply says Christ. The head is Christ, the body is also Christ. And this is the corporate Christ. The Bible mentions the name of "Christian"—that is, "Christ-man" or "Christ-one"—but never does it say "Jesus-man". For the Christian is a part of Christ. "Jesus" refers to His experience on earth as the Son of Man. His life is most marvelous but it is beyond the touch or reach of men. But we *are* Christians, Christ-men. The head is Christ, the body is also Christ. If we understand what Christ is, we will know how very deep is our union with Him. The head is Christ, so also the body is Christ. Were a man's small finger to be broken off, the man would have a scar or blemish on him. By the same token, if a Christian could perish, then Christ would have a blemish. Once we are in Christ, we are forever in Him. For we read in Ephesians that Christ "might sanctify" the church, "having cleansed it by the washing of the water with the word, that he might present the church to himself a glorious church, not having spot or wrinkle or any such thing; but that it should be holy and without blemish" (5.26,27).

"Jesus" speaks of His own personal experience—God sending Him to be the Savior. So that when the Bible talks of Him as man, it calls Him Jesus and never calls Him Christ. After His resurrection, however, if the Bible does not call Him Christ, it at least will identify Him as Lord. This is to emphasize His resurrection and sovereignty. Although several times in Acts and the Epistles He is referred to as Jesus, on those occasions His humanity is especially in view. For this reason, when we address Him today we should not call Him simply Jesus, but the Lord Jesus.

Question 33

At what moment were we crucified with Christ—between His being nailed upon the cross to His giving up of His breath, or was it at the time He expired?

Answer:

If we have understood Question 32, we can now conclude that we were crucified with Christ at the particular moment when He expired. Because prior to His expiration He was engaged in the work of atonement: He was bearing our sins and dying for us. If it were during these times that we were actually crucified then we would have been sharing in His atoning work and thereafter would have become saviors. This, though, would constitute a grave error. Some have gone to the extent of explaining the matter this way: Since the Lord Jesus was on the cross for six hours and hence did not die at once, our death with the Lord must have also lingered on for those six hours. If such were the case, however, we would have shared with the Lord in His atoning work. God forbid! Our death with the Lord occurred at the moment the Lord gave up His breath. With the result that the suffering was His but the effect is ours. We praise and thank God!

Question 34

What is the difference between the meaning and the effect of the blood with that of the cross? Why does the

Bible never say we shed blood with the Lord, but only says
we were crucified with the Lord?

Answer:

At the outset, we need to address ourselves to the
following question. If our sins have been taken away before
God, why do we still have sin in us? We need to answer
whatever doubt is raised by this question first.

The Bible indicates to us in many places how our Lord
shed blood and in many other places how our Lord was
crucified. Is the meaning and effect of the blood the same as
that of the cross? Are they interchangeable? Can we, for
example, change the reading of Hebrews 9.22—"Apart from
shedding of blood there is no remission"—to "Apart from
being crucified on the cross there is no remission"? Moreover, can we in Romans 6.6 alter the words "Knowing this,
that our old man was crucified with him" to read:
"Knowing this, that our old man shed blood with him"? If
their meanings and effects are the same, then they are
interchangeable. If they are not interchangeable, they must
be different.

Hence what are the meaning and the effect of the
blood? And also, of the cross?

Let us first look at the blood side. The Bible mentions a
great deal about the blood, in over four hundred places in
fact. Why does God require the blood? Why will He slay all
who dare to approach Him without the blood? The
following verse will be helpful: "The life of the flesh is in the
blood; and I have given it to you upon the altar to make
atonement for your souls: for it is the blood that maketh
atonement by reason of the life" (Lev. 17.11). This verse

plainly tells us that the blood is for atonement. Where does it atone? On the altar. The work of the blood is before God, it is not in the first instance directed toward us. The blood atones for us before God that He might reckon our sins as taken away; it does not cleanse the sins inwardly in us.

But, some will ask, does not 1 John 1.7 say that "the blood of Jesus his Son cleanseth us from all sin"? Indeed, that Scripture passage so says, but we still need to remember that the cleansing of sins by the blood always refers to a cleansing before God. What are the words which precede these words in this verse? "But if we walk in the light, as he is in the light, we have fellowship one with another"; and then there follows, "and the blood of Jesus his Son cleanseth us from all sin"—thus showing that the cleansing is before God. The effect of the blood is wholly Godward. It is God who demands the blood, and hence the blood is brought before Him.

Yet some may further inquire about the verse in Hebrews 9 which declares this: "How much more shall the blood of Christ . . . cleanse your conscience" (v.14). Let us realize that the cleansing here refers to the cleansing of the conscience, not the cleansing of the sinful nature. Our sinful nature is never cleansed by the blood. The word of God never says that the blood cleanses the old nature, or the flesh. The blood only cleanses us from our sins before God. It only cleanses our conscience that we may have boldness before Him. "Apart from shedding of blood there is no remission." With the blood sins are forgiven, and therefore we have peace. By the blood of the Lord Jesus we have boldness to enter the holy place through the way which He dedicated for us, that new and living way (Heb. 10.19,20). Hence it is the blood which is brought to heaven; the cross is not brought to heaven. The Bible affirms that the Lord Jesus shed blood, not that we ever shed blood with the Lord.

It is well if we lay hold of this fact that the blood secures for us forgiveness before God because it takes away our sins.

Many people do not have liberty and boldness before God because they misunderstand the effect of the blood, taking it as cleansing the sin within them. As a consequence they fail to see the efficacy of the blood. The cleansing in 1 John 1.7 does not apply to the sin within, as though it cleanses even the root of sin. This verse is only speaking of the cleansing before God. He alone demands the blood; and the blood of the Lord Jesus alone satisfies God's heart. Because of this, we freely draw nigh to Him by the blood at any time. No matter how we feel about our sins—whether they are great or small, rough or refined, forgiveable or unforgiveable—all these sins have been cleansed before God. "Though your sins be as scarlet," says the Bible, "they shall be as white as snow" (Is. 1.18). What does this mean? It means God is able to erase every scar and trace of sins as though you had never sinned. This of course points to your condition before Him. Although you are still no good inside, yet before God your sins are all taken away from before His eyes.

By reading Numbers 20.2–9 and 21.4–9 we can readily perceive how bad was the condition of the children of Israel in the wilderness. They sinned and they murmured against God. Yet what does Numbers 23 say about them? "He hath not beheld iniquity in Jacob; neither hath he seen perverseness in Israel" (v.21). Now this was a reality, for we must notice that the matter of sin is dealt with in two distinct areas: one is before God, the other is in us. The blood cleanses our sins before God so that He sees nothing unrighteous with us.

Does the Bible ever state that we are justified by the cross? Never, because justification is through the blood. With the blood before Him, God is able to justify us. What is this justification, that is, what is this righteousness? This righteousness is that which makes us fit to dwell in heaven together with God. The blood of the Lord Jesus gives us a place in heaven that we may dwell with God. We may enter heaven boldly by the blood. God truly knows how valuable is the blood!

"On this day shall atonement be made for you, to cleanse you; from all your sins shall ye be clean before Jehovah" (Lev. 16.30). This plainly tells us that all sins are cleansed before God, not cleansed within us. As regards us, the blood is confined to the cleansing of our conscience that we may no longer be conscious of sins and that there may therefore be no distance between us and God. The blood clears our conscience from the accusation which stems from all the sins we have committed, but it does not take away our consciousness of the root of sin. In His death the Lord bore our sins before God; hence His blood cleanses us before God. Blood is to atone for our sins; it is not for the purpose of eradicating the sinful nature in us.

In fact, in the phrase "taketh away the sin of the world" of John 1.29 and in the phrase "cleanseth us from all sin" of 1 John 1.7, the word "sin" in both cases is singular in number. This is because as a collective term it refers to the whole problem of sin (for an earlier discussion of this subject see Question 7 above). In neither case can the "taketh away" or "cleanseth us" be applied to the matter of taking away the root of sin or a cleansing us from the root of sin. Both verses are in reference to how the blood of the Lord solves our sin problem.

Moving on next to the second part of the question, we must see that the meaning and the effect of the cross is quite different from that of the blood. Blood is before God, the cross is in us. Blood solves our sin problem, the cross solves the problem of the old man. God has not only given us liberty before Him through the blood, He has also given us the cross that we may have our corrupt self or flesh dealt with.

The flesh is dealt with by the cross: "They that are of Christ Jesus have crucified the flesh with the passions and the lusts thereof" (Gal. 5.24). Does it say the blood cleanses the flesh? No, it says crucified the flesh. Cleansing is of no avail here. Let us illustrate it this way. Both a living child and a clay doll become dirty. After the living child is washed he is clean. But no matter how the clay doll is washed it is never clean because it is made of clay. The corrupted flesh is like the clay doll. It has become so corrupted throughout that even the blood of the Lord cannot cleanse it. The only way to deal with the flesh is to have it crucified.

God uses the blood to cleanse us from our sins, but He uses the cross to crucify our flesh. We cannot have our sins cleansed before God by the cross, nor can we cleanse our flesh by the blood. "Knowing this, that our old man was crucified with him, that the body of sin might be done away, that so we should no longer be in bondage to sin" (Rom. 6.6). In the original Greek, "done away" in this passage and "cumber" in Luke 13.7 are the same word. It does not mean an annihilating of the body of sin, rather does it signify rendering it useless or powerless. It can therefore also be translated as "unemployed". After God has crucified the old man, the body which always is in subjection to sin is rendered powerless, and thus is no longer in bondage to sin—just as if it were unemployed. We Christians ought not to sin; yet the way of victory lies not in our own conception but according to the word of God. Today we need not ask Him to do the work of sanctification for us, we are instead to thank Him that He has already crucified us on the cross. We need not to believe that God will do but to believe that He has done it. While promise is to be obtained through prayer, fact is to be gained through simple faith. The crucifixion of the old man with the Lord is an accomplished fact. It is well if we believe it. Simply believe, and no temptation can then touch us. The only way of victory is to abide in the Lord by faith, abiding in the accomplished fact in the Lord. Any deviation will curtail the progress.

"I have been crucified with Christ" (Gal. 2.20). Here it does not declare that I have shed blood with Christ. Instead it announces that this no good I of mine has been crucified with Christ. Let us be absolutely clear: the blood deals with sins, the cross deals with the flesh. The blood gives us forgiveness and acquittal; the cross gives us release and deliverance from the power of sin that we may no longer be in bondage to sin. Blood is related to salvation, the cross is linked to victory. Blood solves our sins before God; the cross dissolves our very selves. Just as we believe in the blood let us also believe in the cross. And it is well if we believe in both daily.

"Even so reckon ye also yourselves to be dead unto sin, but alive unto God in Christ Jesus" (Rom. 6.11). "Neither present your members unto sin as instruments of unrighteousness; but . . . your members as instruments of righteousness unto God" (v.13). We now are doing two things: the one is to stand daily on verse 11, believing that we have died and that therefore the body of sin has become unemployed; the other is to present our members as instruments of righteousness to God. If our presenting is inadequate, we will yet fall. If we do not do what God wants us to do, we still may falter. We must trust on the one hand and obey on the other. Trusting what has already been accomplished and obeying what God is asking will spontaneously bring in victory.

Question 35

The Bible declares that the Lord Jesus died for all. If a person does not believe in the Lord Jesus, will he perish?

Answer:

"The love of Christ constraineth us; because we thus judge, that one died for all, therefore all died" (2 Cor. 5.14). The "one" here is Christ. The "all" whom He died for are all men. Now it may appear from this, therefore, that even though a person does not believe in the Lord Jesus, he should not die. Yet in John we read that "he that believeth not hath been judged already, because he hath not believed on the name of the only begotten Son of God" (3.18). What can be said about the righteousness of God and His way of operation? Let us look into this matter.

"The Son of man came not to be ministered unto, but to minister, and to give his life a ransom for many" (Matt. 20.28). "Who gave himself a ransom for all" (1 Tim. 2.6). What is the difference between "many" and "all"? The "many" in the first passage includes all who believe, and the Lord Jesus has died for all the many who believe in Him. The "all" in the second passage refers to all men, for whom the Lord Jesus has prepared a ransom. The "for" in Matthew carries in it the idea of substituting, while the "for" in 1 Timothy conveys the idea of providing. With respect to the believers, the Lord Jesus has died to substitute His death for their death as well as to provide for them a ransom. With respect to sinners, however, His death has provided for them a ransom, though it does not serve to substitute for their death. Hence the scope of substitution before God is limited.

The words "one died for all" in 2 Corinthians 5.14 means to say that one had died on behalf of all. It means that the death of the Lord Jesus has provided sufficiently for the use of all men. So far as provision is concerned the death of the Lord Jesus *is* for all men so that all may have the opportunity to be saved. Only for the believers would the word "substitute" be used.

"He is the propitiation for our sins; and not for ours only, but also for the whole world" (1 John 2.2). Christ is the propitiation for the unbelievers as well as for the believers. But again the meaning here is not substitution, but provision. The salvation of God has already been prepared. When you receive it you then will be reckoned by God as being one among the "many". Christ died on behalf of all men, since His death has made provision for all men; but it cannot be taken to mean a substitution in death for all men. If anyone does not believe, he will perish. This is man's responsibility before God.*

Question 36

How do you reconcile "nor of the will of man" (John 1.13) with "he that will" (Rev. 22.17) in regard to eternal life?

---

* "I may observe once for all, that in the usage of these two words, as applied to our redemption by Christ, *all* is the objective, *many* the subjective designation of those for whom Christ died." Henry Alford, *The Greek Testament* (Chicago: Moody Press, 1968), Vol. I, p. 206.—*Translator*

Answer:

To this agelong question theologians hold opposite views. Some maintain that our salvation is purely a matter of man's will, others insist that our salvation is wholly a matter of God's will. Let us acknowledge, however, that God's truth often has two sides. If we are not careful we can easily become unbalanced. People usually tend to go to extremes.

Is salvation entirely a matter of man's will or a matter of God's will? Actually both wills are involved. Had it not been God's will to save, no one could be saved. But at the same time God's will is of no avail if man himself is not willing. God is willing, yet man too must be willing. "How often would I have gathered thy children together", said the Lord Jesus, "even as a hen gathereth her own brood under her wings, and ye would not!" (Luke 13.34) This is the two sides of God's truth. Both must be willing; to have only the one side will not be successful. If we wish to know the truth we must not hold on to only one side. In tempting the Lord Jesus Satan said this to Him: "For it is written"; but the Lord's answer was this: "Again it is written" (Matt. 4.6,7). True, it is written, but attention should also be paid to the again it is written. It is not adequate to just lay hold of a verse or a few verses and try to prove one side of the truth, for there may be many other verses which will prove the other side of the truth. For example, to say that a Christian once saved is forever saved is to declare but one side of the truth. For at the same time, if a Christian after he is saved should keep on sinning without exercising any repentance, he will most certainly be *punished*. Though he will not be punished with the second death *itself*, nevertheless, as the Scripture says, he will "be *hurt* of the second death" (Rev. 2.11). Let us recognize that this too is truth.

People will ask why on the one hand the Bible says "he that will, let him take the water of life freely" and "whosoever believeth on him should not perish, but have eternal life", and on the other hand it says that one's salvation is predestinated by God? Someone has answered this question quite well. This person's answer runs something like this: On the outside of the door of heaven there is written the words "Whosoever will may come" (Rev. 22.17) and hence whosoever wills to do so may enter. But upon entering through the door of heaven he looks back and sees written on the inside of the door: "Chosen from before the foundation of the earth" (Eph. 1.4). Such a reply shows the two sides of God's truth. And our own experience indeed bears this out. At the moment of believing, belief is all which is required. Yet having believed, one reminisces why *he* is saved whereas many others who are far better than he are not saved. He acknowledges that he is ignorant and cannot explain. He can only say that his salvation is predestinated by God.

Whosoever believes shall be saved. This is the word to unbelievers. But God's election—God's predestination—is the word for believers. It will be unwise, if not a grave error, if the word for believers is spoken to unbelievers. Please note, for instance, that it was to the *disciples* that the Lord asserted: "Ye did not choose me, but I chose you" (John 15.16). These words should therefore not be told to unbelievers.

Once a theological student went to see a servant of God, asking: "I find the Bible saying that man's salvation is predestinated by God. Yet as I am preaching, I look at someone's face and conclude that God has not predestinated *him* to be saved. What, then, will happen if I do persuade that one to get saved?" The servant of God wisely answered: "You go and preach. And if you persuade anyone to be saved, then he must have indeed been predestinated by God."

We ought to realize that the reason why God tells the believers that they are predestinated to be saved is for the purpose of arousing in them a heart of gratitude such as might be expressed by some believer in the following way: "Many are still unsaved; and yet here I am, saved. I can only say that God has chosen me out of the tens of thousands. Hallelujah! I am saved, not because of my merit but because of God himself. I can do nothing but thank and praise Him!"

Hence we may answer that the words in Revelation 22.17 are spoken to unbelievers. And in this way shall the truth be balanced.

Question 37

Does not Luke 10.25–37 indicate that if a person should love the Lord his God with all his heart and with all his soul and with all his strength and with all his mind and should also love his neighbor as himself, he will inherit eternal life? If so, is not eternal life obtained by works?

Answer:

The Bible tells us that eternal life is given according to faith, not according to works. In the entire New Testament there are over five hundred instances where words such as "Believe . . . shalt be saved", "Believe . . . hath eternal life", "Believe . . . shalt be justified", etc., are used. The lawyer in Luke 10 asked, "What shall I do to inherit eternal life?" But the Lord asked in return, "What is written in the law? how readest thou?" (vv.25,26) And he answered, "Thou shalt love the Lord thy God with all thy heart, and with all thy soul, and with all thy strength, and with all thy mind; and thy neighbor as thyself" (v.27). Then the Lord said, "Thou hast answered right: this do, and thou shalt live" (v.28). The law teaches two things: (1) to love God, and (2) to love people. Since these are all works, does it not appear to be that eternal life is obtained by works? If the story had ended here at verse 28 the issue of eternal life would in truth be a puzzle. But thank God, the story continues on to verse 37.

The lawyer asked, "And who is my neighbor?" (v.29) By this he meant to say that he knew God but he knew not who his neighbor was. In response to this question the Lord spoke of a man fallen into the hands of robbers on his way to Jericho. A priest passed by without saving him; so did a Levite go by without offering any help. Only a Samaritan came to save him and save him to the uttermost. Then the Lord asked that lawyer, "Which of these three, thinkest thou, proved neighbor unto him that fell among the robbers?" (v.36) Let us notice that the question asked by the lawyer was, "Who is my neighbor?" Our Lord's question in verse 36 was, "Which of these three, thinkest thou, proved neighbor unto him that fell among the robbers?" What the Lord meant was this: You are the one who has fallen into robbers' hands; now then, which one of these three is your neighbor? "He that showed mercy on him," replied the lawyer. Whereupon the Lord answered, "Go, and do thou likewise". We are plainly shown that the Lord had not asked the lawyer to go and be a good Samaritan; instead, He caused the lawyer to know that his neighbor was the good Samaritan. In other words, it was the Samaritan who saved him. In short, this good Samaritan was the savior of the lawyer.

He who falls in the hands of robbers is a sinner. Neither the priest nor the Levite can be his savior. A sinner's neighbor is the sinner's savior. To love the neighbor is to love the Savior. To have eternal life is to trust in the Savior; to have eternal life is not to trust in oneself as a savior. Many have misread this parable, thinking erroneously that it teaches us to treat people well. Yet the Lord has never said, Let the one who falls among robbers be his own savior; on the contrary, He is saying here that you have fallen into the hands of the robbers and the good Samaritan who saves you is your neighbor and that therefore you ought to love him always. He whom we know not comes to save us. Hence the neighbor to be loved is the Lord Jesus himself.

People love the Lord because they have eternal life; they do not get eternal life because they love the Lord. There is first the neighbor relationship, then the affection. This passage of Scripture shows us several things: (1) man is fallen, (2) he cannot save himself, (3) the Savior has already come, and (4) if anyone accepts His salvation, that person will be saved and will in turn love Him. The mistake many commit is in trying to make themselves their own savior. They do not know the gospel of grace. We ought to realize that the Lord wants us to love the good Samaritan, who is none other than the Lord himself.

Question 38

In Luke 16 we have the story of the rich man and Lazarus. Did the rich man perish because he had received

good things in his lifetime whereas Lazarus was saved
because he had received evil things in his life? Or is there
some other cause?

Answer:

Some maintain that the rich man perished because he
had enjoyed good things in his lifetime but that Lazarus
was saved since he had suffered evil. They base their
conclusion on the words of Abraham to the rich man
recorded in Luke 16.25. Is this so? As a matter of fact, in
verse 25 Abraham was merely comparing the respective
conditions of the rich man and Lazarus before and after
death. It is only with verse 29 that we have given to us the
basic reason for perdition or salvation. Let us take careful
note of it: "But Abraham saith, They have Moses and the
prophets, let them hear them." This reveals that the rich
man perished because he had not heard Moses and the
Prophets, whereas Lazarus was saved because he *did* hear
Moses and the Prophets.

What are the words of Moses and the Prophets? After
His resurrection the Lord fell into conversation with those
two disciples who were on their way to Emmaus, and Luke
in 24.27 makes this interesting comment: "Beginning from
Moses and from all the prophets," the Lord Jesus "inter-
preted to them in all the scriptures the things concerning
himself". And the same night He appeared to His disciples
in Jerusalem and He said to them: "These are my words
which I spake unto you, while I was yet with you, that all
things must needs be fulfilled, which are written in the law
of Moses, and the prophets, and the psalms, concerning me.
Then opened he their mind, that they might understand

the scriptures; and he said unto them, Thus it is written, that the Christ should suffer, and rise again from the dead the third day" (Luke 24.44–46). Accordingly, the words of Moses and the Prophets mean all the words which are spoken concerning the Lord Jesus. In other words, the rich man perished because he had not accepted the Savior who died and was raised from the dead for him, while Lazarus was saved because he had accepted the Savior.

God has already given us the Bible. Our therefore having the words of the Scriptures to believe, He will not send a man who is raised from the dead to preach the gospel (Luke 16.31). He has hidden himself to such a degree that men begin to imagine there is no God. Even though people sin so terribly, they will not be instantly stricken to death by lightning. They can continually blaspheme God and still not receive immediate judgment from Him. God has not arranged the stars in heaven to spell out the truth of His existence or the sin of mankind; He does not use spectacular ways to prove himself; He simply wants men to believe in His word.

"And he said unto him, If they hear not Moses and the prophets, neither will they be persuaded, if one rise from the dead" (Luke 16.31). Here is given to us a revelation, which is, that if people do not believe in Moses and the Prophets they will not be persuaded even if someone is raised from the dead. Whoever does not accept the witness of the Bible will still not believe even should one rise from the dead.

Question 39

Romans 4 says Abraham was justified by faith, while

James 2 says Abraham was justified by works. How do we explain these two justifications? What is their relationship to each other?

Answer:

Concerning justification, the Bible shows us two different kinds: one is justification by faith, the other is justification by works. We may prove them with the following passages from the Scriptures.

"By him [the Lord Jesus] every one that believeth is justified from all things, from which ye could not be justified by the law of Moses" (Acts 13.39). "We reckon therefore that a man is justified by faith apart from the works of the law" (Rom. 3.28). In both passages Paul speaks of the justification by faith.

"I know nothing against myself; yet am I not hereby justified: but he that judgeth me is the Lord" (1 Cor. 4.4). What is said here is basically different from the above two passages. For Paul is here speaking about being rewarded at the judgment seat of Christ. What is meant by "justified" in this 1 Corinthians verse? It means reward through having performed good works. Thus Paul mentions justification by faith on the one hand and justification by works on the other.

We know that the two Pauline letters of Romans and Galatians speak of justification by faith whereas James speaks of justification by works. Some people have speculated that in view of the apparent inadequacy of justification by faith as explained by Paul, James intends to fill up the lack by speaking on justification by works. But such a concept is most inaccurate. For when James wrote his epistle Paul had yet to write Romans and Galatians.

In Romans Paul tells us that we are justified by faith. He is afraid that some are ignorant of what God has done and of what Christ has accomplished and what the efficacy of the blood is, thereby considering faith by itself as inadequate and advocating the addition of man's works in order to be saved. To refute such a misconcept Paul quotes the story of Abraham to prove that justification is indeed by faith. But James also quotes Abraham, yet he does so in speaking of justification by works. Hence we can assume that there must be an intimate relationship between faith and works in the matter of justification. What both Paul and James speak of is actually one thing. Let us now see what is the inner relationship between the two and how they are related.

First, let us consider Romans 4:—"If Abraham was justified by works, he hath whereof to glory; but not toward God. For what saith the scripture? And Abraham believed God, and it was reckoned unto him for righteousness" (vv.2,3). "Is this blessing then pronounced upon the circumcision, or upon the uncircumcision also? for we say, To Abraham his faith was reckoned for righteousness. How then was it reckoned? when he was in circumcision, or in uncircumcision? Not in circumcision, but in uncircumcision" (vv.9,10). We see from this that Abraham was justified before he received circumcision. Now the Jews look upon circumcision as one of the most important works of its kind. They look down upon the uncircumcised gentiles as pigs and dogs. But before Abraham himself was circumcised, he was justified by faith.

"And he received the sign of circumcision, a seal of the righteousness of the faith which he had while he was in uncircumcision: that he might be the father of all them that believe, though they be in uncircumcision, that righteousness might be reckoned unto them" (v.11). Circumcision is like a seal stamped by God, declaring that now is one justified by faith and there will be no change forever. God told Abraham to be circumcised, yet not that he might thus be justified but that there might be a seal put upon him, thus showing how unchangeable is justification by faith. Even if later on Abraham should decline to offer Isaac, he was still justified by faith. Let us therefore rest in peace, knowing that justification by faith is sure and secure.

"And the father of circumcision to them who not only are of the circumcision, but who also walk in the steps of that faith of our father Abraham which he had in uncircumcision" (v.12). This verse indicates to us that the circumcised must also have faith, since Abraham himself was justified by faith before being circumcised.

Romans proves to us that a sinner cannot be justified by works of the law. Galatians shows us that a believer cannot be sanctified by works of the law. We are sanctified by faith as well as justified by faith. How can we begin in the Spirit and try to be perfected in the flesh? In any case, the seal has already been put on us. So then, they that are of faith are blessed with the faithful Abraham.

Now let us turn to James 2:—"What doth it profit, my brethren, if a man say he hath faith, but have not works? can that faith save him?" (v.14) What is the motive behind these words written by James? To whom does he address himself? For some people boast that they have faith, yet there is no work displayed in their lives. If they are not refuted, the church will be evilly affected. Faith should be kept before God, not to be bragged about before men. Faith needs to be accomplished by works. All who say they have faith and yet have no works cannot be saved by their kind of faith.

"Saved" in the Scriptures has several meanings. "I know," says Paul, "that this shall turn out to my salvation, through your supplication and the supply of the Spirit of Jesus Christ" (Phil. 1.19). Is not Paul already saved? This obviously does not refer to a believer's receiving eternal life; it points to Paul's being released from prison. "Who delivered us out of so great a death, and will deliver: on whom we have set our hope that he will also still deliver us" (2 Cor. 1.10), declares Paul once more. Some think that this alludes to how the Lord died on the cross to save us from the penalty of sin and is now our Advocate in heaven saving us from the power of sin and in the future will come again to save our body. Who knows for sure, say they, that these matters are not what Paul in fact is talking about here? Well, the deliverances herein mentioned pertain to Paul's and his friends' physical deliverances by the Lord. For by reading the entire context we learn how they had formerly been aflicted in Asia to the point of despairing even of life but that the Lord delivered them out of such a situation. For this reason, Paul believed that the Lord would deliver him out of afflictions yet further—both now and in the future.

In like manner the word "save" used by James above has reference to being profited through environment. This is clear if we read the verses which follow: "If a brother or sister be naked and in lack of daily food, and one of you say unto them, Go in peace, be ye warmed and filled; and yet ye give them not the things needful to the body; what doth it profit?" (James 2.15,16) The "one of you" points to those who brag emptily of having faith. They do not supply food and dress to the brothers and sisters in need, but instead they vainly pronounce to the needy: Go in peace. The problem involved here is not one of going to heaven, but is one that is concerned with the warmth and the filling up of

the body today. What James means to say is that you
cannot simply say you have faith and yet do not supply the
needs of your brothers and sisters.

"Even so faith, if it have not works, is dead in itself"
(v.17). This is a verdict given by James. He means that if
you believe that those needy ones will be warmed and filled
and yet you do not lend a hand to supply their needs, such
kind of faith without works is not faith at all; it is dead. A
living faith believes in the heart that the God of mercy
would not permit those needy brethren to go cold or
hungry; and at the same time this living faith causes us to
distribute various physical supplies to them.

"Yea, a man will say, Thou hast faith, and I have
works: show me thy faith apart from thy works, and I by
works will show thee my faith" (v.18). Those who brag
vainly of their faith will be challenged by others, who will
say: You say you have faith but where do you express it?
You can only say with your mouth; you will not even lift a
finger at the time of real need. Where then *is* your faith?
You pretend to believe for others, though you yourself have
not faith. If you have faith, why do you not give all that you
have? Your brother or sister is now naked and in lack of
daily food. Why do you not give what you have to him since
you yourself are warmly clothed and well-fed? You say you
have faith, but how are you going to prove your faith? But
as a matter of fact, your faith is but empty word, your faith
is dead. It does not profit the needy ones. On the other
hand, though, I have works, and by my supplying the needs
of brothers and sisters I prove my faith. I believe that God
would not cause us to suffer cold or hunger, therefore when
I see the needs of brothers and sisters around me I share all
that I have with them. My works are based on my faith. My
works are the expressions of my faith. By my works I show
forth my faith.

"Thou believest that God is one; thou doest well: the demons also believe, and shudder" (v.19). The children of Israel believe in one God, and this is right. But the demons believe also in one God, yet they remain as demons. What James infers from this fact is that faith without works is like demons who remain demons though believing in God.

"But wilt thou know, O vain man, that faith apart from works is barren?" (v.20) Vain man is but another name for the one who brags emptily of his faith. It can be said that he really does not have faith in his heart. Only he who supplies others in a practical way can demonstrate his faith to people. First faith, then works. True faith produces true works. The one who boasts of his faith yet has no works is proven to have a dead faith. Since his heart errs before God, his faith is also dead.

"Was not Abraham our father justified by works, in that he offered up Isaac his son upon the altar?" (v.21) If James had not quoted the story of Abraham, some readers of Romans and Galatians would consider outright that James is in error in what he says, for had not Paul spoken of justification by faith, and therefore faith is sufficient without the need of works? Yet what James maintains is that Abraham was indeed justified by faith but he was also justified by works. James does not overturn Abraham's being justified by faith; he only proves by his offering up of Isaac that Abraham's work is the expression of Abraham's faith. So that he was not only justified by faith but also justified by works.

Instead of overturning justification by faith, James actually strengthens it with justification by works in proving what true faith is. Abraham's offering up of Isaac is a work, and this work is reckoned to him as righteousness. But what kind of work is it? It is a work of faith. "By faith, Abraham, being tried, offered up Issac: yea, he that had gladly

received the promises was offering up his only begotten son;
even he to whom it was said, In Isaac shall thy seed be
called: accounting that God is able to raise up, even from
the dead; from whence he did also in a figure receive him
back" (Heb. 11.17–19). In quoting the offering up of Isaac
by Abraham, James shows us that true faith must be
accompanied by works. Abraham gladly received the
promises of God. He believed in what God had told him,
notably that "in Isaac shall thy seed be called" (v.18).
Eliezer was not the one, nor was Ishmael, nor was any son
who might later be born of Sarah; Isaac alone was to be the
heir of the inheritance and the promises.

Now God tested Abraham in order to see what his heart
was toward God and how real was his faith. God asked him
to offer up on the altar his son Isaac—the one who was
divinely appointed to be his heir—and there to be slain and
burnt. Yet how would God's promise ever be fulfilled if
Abraham loved God and burned Isaac? If he wanted to
fulfill God's promise he could not comply with God's
request. According to man these two, far from being
unified, are contradictory to each other. Yet to a living faith
they are unified and not contradictory. It is God who
promises, and it is God who requires. God will never
contradict himself. Between promise and request God will
open a new way, that is to say, the way of resurrection:
"accounting that God is able to raise up, even from the
dead" (v.19).

Abraham's faith is thus defined: Even though I slay
Isaac and offer him as a burnt-offering, I still believe Your
promised word—"in Isaac shall thy seed be called"—will be
fulfilled, for you shall raise up Isaac from the dead. So when
he went off to the appointed place to offer up Isaac, he went
with a determined heart. He actually bound Isaac and
raised high his knife. His heart toward God was absolute,

there being no reservation. His faith in God was firm and void of doubt. And when the angel of the Lord called to him and said, "Lay not thy hand upon the lad, neither do thou any thing unto him" (Gen. 22.12), he "did also in a figure receive him back" (Heb. 11.19). Abraham's offering up of his only begotten son was a work of faith. And this is called justification by works.

"Thou seest that faith wrought with his works, and by works was faith made perfect" (James 2.22). This continues on from the preceding thought. Due to the fact that by offering up Isaac on the altar Abraham was justified by works, we come to realize that faith runs parallel with works, or, to phrase it another way, that faith and works operate together. Abraham's work is performed through his faith, and faith is perfected by his works. A faith which has not been tested is undependable. By his offering Isaac, Abraham's faith is both proven and perfected.

"And the scripture was fulfilled which saith, And Abraham believed God, and it was reckoned unto him for righteousness; and he was called the friend of God" (v.23). "Abraham believed God, and it was reckoned unto him for righteousness"—this word is recorded in Genesis 15.6. What is the relationship between the offering up of Isaac in Genesis 22 to that word? Why should James quote it in his epistle when he suggests that the offering up of Isaac is a justification by works? And he even adds that the scripture was fulfilled. The relationship is simply this: that justification by works fulfills justification by faith. It appears as though justification by faith is a prophecy and that justification by works is the fulfillment of that prophecy. He who has faith must have works, for works explain the reality of faith. Abraham believed in God, he was reckoned as righteous, and he was also called the friend of God. Hence Abraham's work in offering up Isaac is the fulfillment of

Abraham's faith in God. In short, his offering up of Isaac demonstrates to us his faith in God.

"Ye see that by works a man is justified, and not only by faith" (v.24). Since Genesis 22 is the fulfillment of Genesis 15, and since works are the expressions of faith because faith without works is dead and faith is made perfect by works, therefore a man is justified by works and not only by faith. Let us notice that James has not said that a man is justified by works and not by faith; he merely says that a man is justified by works and not *only* by faith. And by this he means to say that after a man is justified by faith he needs to prove and to be made perfect in that faith through justification by works, even as Abraham after he was justified by faith was tested by God and thus was justified by works.

"And in like manner was not also Rahab the harlot justified by works, in that she received the messengers, and sent them out another way?" (v.25) James first cites an excellent person such as Abraham to show that he was not only justified by faith but also justified by works. Next, though, he cites a bad woman such as Rahab to show that she too was justified by works. For she received the messengers and sent them out another way. What kind of work is this work? "By faith Rahab the harlot perished not with them that were disobedient, having received the spies with peace" (Heb. 11.31). This work is also a work of faith. Faith and works are inseparable; they are the two sides of one thing. With respect to this one and same thing it is called faith in Hebrews and works in James. Works are the expressions of faith whereas faith is the source of works. To say that there is faith and yet there be no works of faith shown, that faith is dead. Consequently, after there is a justification by faith there must also be the justification by works.

"For as the body apart from the spirit is dead, even so faith apart from works is dead" (v.26). In Chapter 2, from verse 14 onward, James speaks of the relationship between faith and works. There is a kind of faith which has no works, being nothing but a vain boast; and it is dead. But there is another kind of faith which has works; and it is living. Works prove the faith, and works make perfect the faith. James uses what Abraham and Rahab did as evidences to prove his point. And finally, he uses this other illustration: "As the body apart from the spirit is dead, even so faith apart from works is dead": living faith is always accompanied by works: so that just as the body without the spirit is dead, faith without works is also dead.

Question 40

Why does Luke 15 use three parables? Would not one parable have been sufficient?

Answer:

In Luke 15 we find three parables which all have reference to the matter of being "lost". The first parable speaks of a lost sheep; the second, a lost piece of silver; and the third, a lost son. Many who read this chapter are surprised at its use of the "lost" to signify a sinner, and puzzled as to why the Lord would tell as many as three parables instead of just one. We should know, however, that the purpose of the parables here spoken by the Lord Jesus is not to describe the lost or the fall of man; instead, His emphasis is on how God treats a lost soul. If He intended only to speak of the lost, then of course one parable would be quite sufficient. But the Lord lays stress on how God treats the lost, and therefore none of these three parables may be omitted. Toward the lost, the Triune God with Father, Son and Holy Spirit have their respective work. And these three parables do indeed reveal the three-sided work of the Triune God.

Can the order of these three parables be changed? No, for the gospel would be tampered with were we to disturb their order. For in these three parables we are given the order of the plan of God's redemption. The first one speaks of the work of the Lord Jesus as the Good Shepherd. John 10 tells us that the good shepherd lays down his life for the sheep. Next, the Lord mentions the parable of the woman who sought diligently for the lost piece of silver. The good shepherd seeks his lost sheep in a different place from that of the woman who seeks for her lost piece of silver. The good shepherd goes outside his house to seek the sheep. And so does the Lord Jesus, who left His Father's house and came to the world to seek each one of us. The woman, though, searches for her lost coin inside the house. She lights a lamp, sweeps the house, and seeks diligently for the lost piece. Do we see the order here? First comes the Lord Jesus to accomplish redemption, then the Holy Spirit enlightens us within that we may accept what the Lord Jesus has accomplished. The Bible shows us *two* wonderful gifts of God, not just one. He gives us His own Son, and He gives us the Holy Spirit.

Some preachers commit a serious mistake by preaching only half the gospel. They merely tell people: "God so loved the world, that he gave his only begotten Son, that whosoever believeth on him should not perish, but have eternal life" (John 3.16); but they then fail to tell what the Lord Jesus has said: "I will pray the Father, and he shall give you another Comforter, that he may be with you for ever" (John 14.16). God has not only sent the Lord Jesus as the Good Shepherd who comes and seeks us out, but He has also sent the Holy Spirit to enlighten us. In the first parable there is no lamp; in the second, there is a lamp. The first parable speaks of seeking outside the house; the second speaks of searching within the house. The Lord Jesus goes to the outside of the house—the world—to seek the lost sheep; the Holy Spirit is in the house—within us—enlightening us with the lamp of light and seeking diligently for the lost piece of silver. But finally, the last parable speaks of the father who waits for his son to return home. The Savior having come to seek and the Holy Spirit having come to search (for what the Lord has done is not in vain, nor can the work of the Holy Spirit be fruitless), God is now waiting at home for the son to come back.

If either the first or the second parable is missing, the third parable cannot stand. For without the coming of the Good Shepherd to lay down His life for the sheep, redemption will not be accomplished. And without the enlightening of the Holy Spirit, none will be convicted of sin, of righteousness, and of judgment. Although some people may experience partial conviction over their sins, no one can truly repent without the enlightenment of the Holy Spirit.

If the Good Shepherd does not lay down His life for the sheep, the Father cannot receive the prodigal son when he returns home. The work of the Holy Spirit is based on the death of the Lord. If the Lord did not die, the heavenly Father could not forgive man's sins; else God would be unrighteous. Let us lay hold of the fact that God's forgiveness is God's righteousness. He loves us, but His love comes through His righteousness; otherwise He would be found to be unrighteous by doing something against His righteous nature. Without the shedding of blood there can be no remission of sins. If it were possible to receive forgiveness without the shed blood of the Lord, it would be the same as telling people that we do not need the Savior. How are we saved? Truly we have sinned, but equally true is it that the Savior has borne our sins. We may therefore boldly approach God and be accepted. If we do not have a Savior our conscience will never be at peace. Since the Lord Jesus has died and has accomplished redemption, the heavenly Father is now waiting to receive us. We should notice that when the prodigal son returned home his father did not utter a word of blame nor a word of exhortation. This is because the Savior has already accomplished redemption for him and the Holy Spirit has also enlightened him so that his sins are forgiven and washed with the blood.

But we also need to recognize the importance of the second parable. For even though the Lord Jesus as the Good Shepherd comes and dies and the heavenly Father is found waiting at home, the prodigal son will still be unable to return if there is not the enlightening of the Holy Spirit. It is the Holy Spirit who convicts him of sin and as to why he does not believe in the Lord earlier. It is the Holy Spirit who convinces him of righteousness because the Lord has already been resurrected and has ascended and been accepted by God, and so prompts him as to why he does not receive the Lord Jesus. It is the Holy Spirit who demonstrates to him the matter of judgment since Satan has already been judged and is no longer man's master, and therefore asks why he still follows Satan. All these works are done by the Holy Spirit. For this reason we must pay attention to what the Holy Spirit will do as well as to the matter of believing in what the Lord Jesus has done.

Some people emphasize what the Holy Spirit will do

but overlook what Christ has done, whereas other people pay attention to what Christ has done and forget what the Holy Spirit will do. Those whose sole attention is focused on what Christ has done will maintain that since Christ has died and been resurrected and has accomplished all things, the Holy Spirit in leading us into all truth merely causes us to know these facts of Christ's death, resurrection, and glorification. But those whose interest lies only in what the Holy Spirit will do will assert that with the Holy Spirit performing a special work in us we will have a special experience. Both these classes of people are partially inclined. We know that a bird has two wings. If one of its wings is clipped it cannot fly. These two classes of men wish to clip away one of the wings of God's truth. If a person's attention is riveted solely on what the Holy Spirit will do, He will be without a foundation or ground, because the work of the Holy Spirit can only be based on the finished work of Christ.

"The grace of the Lord Jesus Christ, and the love of God, and the communion of the Holy Spirit, be with you all" (2 Cor. 13.14). God's heart is love; it is God who initiates the plan to save us. But love is something inward; its outward expression is grace. Love expressed is grace, and inside grace is love. The reason the grace of the Lord Jesus is first mentioned in the verse is because redemption is accomplished by Christ. It is God who loves, and this love as shown in Christ becomes grace. The Holy Spirit communicates to us that which Christ has accomplished, and so it is termed the communion of the Holy Spirit. The Holy Spirit himself has nothing to give; He simply communicates to us what Christ has done. Without the Holy Spirit we are unable to receive the grace of the Lord. Yet neither are we able to receive anything if we merely want the Holy Spirit and do not desire what Christ has accomplished. A water pipe is for conducting water. Neither water without a pipe nor a pipe without water is effectual. Let us see, then, that the three parables in Luke 15 are not repetitions, for they do show forth the order of God's plan of redemption. Christ accomplishes redemption, the Holy Spirit enlightens, and God the Father receives us with His love. A right understanding of these three parables will give us a balanced Christian life.

Question 41

What is the relationship between the death of the Lord Jesus and the descending of the Holy Spirit?

Answer:

This question has great significance in salvation and the gospel; therefore it must be investigated.

A great number of people have an erroneous concept about the Holy Spirit. They think that to be filled with the Holy Spirit costs a great deal and requires much self-denial and hard pleading until they feel elated, and that only then will they be able to be good Christians as well as to have power to preach the gospel. But in carefully reading the Bible we do not find this to be the case. Instead, the Bible tells us that the only cost for having the Holy Spirit has been paid by the Lord Jesus Christ. Because of the death and resurrection of the Lord Jesus, God has given the Holy Spirit. The descent of the Spirit is due to the death, the blood, and the merit of the Lord Jesus and not due in any way to what price or merit we pay or obtain.

While the Lord Jesus was on earth He told the disciples
that the Father would give the Holy Spirit to those who
asked Him (Luke 11.13), for at that time the Holy Spirit
had not yet come. But after His resurrection He "breathed
on" the disciples "and saith unto them, Receive ye the Holy
Spirit" (John 20.22). Henceforth it is no longer a matter of
asking for the Holy Spirit but of receiving the Holy Spirit.

A servant of God once put it this way. "The Holy Spirit
has already descended. Now if the water pipe for the Holy
Spirit is blocked, remove the cork and the water will flow.
We must not consecrate ourselves just once, but should do it
often." On the basis of the Lord's blood, death, resurrection,
and ascension, the Holy Spirit has already come. The
problem today is to remove the cork by consecrating
ourselves to the Lord and so we shall be filled with the Holy
Spirit. Consecration is the way to the filling or inflow of the
Holy Spirit, while the blood of the Lord is the basis for the
outflow of the Holy Spirit. If we wish to be filled with the
Spirit we need to consecrate ourselves. The more thorough
our consecration the fuller the filling of the Holy Spirit. The
blood of the Lord Jesus, on the other hand, is that which
gives water to the pipe; that is to say, it gives us the Holy
Spirit.

It is recorded in the Old Testament that while the
children of Israel were in the wilderness Moses smote the
rock with the staff and water flowed out of the rock. First
Corinthians 10 says that "the rock was Christ" (v.4). The
outflow of the Holy Spirit is not caused by our consecration
but depends on the death of the Lord Jesus. In Leviticus 14,
according to the law of the leper in the day of his cleansing,
he shall have the blood of the trespass-offering put upon the
tip of his right ear, the thumb of his right hand, and the
great toe of his right foot before he has the oil in the left
hand of the priest put upon the tip of his right ear, the

thumb of his right hand, and the great toe of his right foot and the rest of the oil put upon his head. The blood here points to redemption, while the oil points to the Holy Spirit. The Holy Spirit comes upon the leper not because he himself declares that he is well but because he is cleansed by the blood, and only then is he anointed with oil.

Our ear is to listen to God's voice, our hand is to do His work, and our foot is to walk in His path. All these must first be cleansed by the blood. On the basis of the redemptive work of the Lord we have our sins washed by His blood, and then we shall be filled with the Holy Spirit who gives us power to live and to work.

The New Testament speaks more clearly on this matter than does the Old Testament:

> Now on the last day, the great day of the feast, Jesus stood and cried, saying, If any man thirst, let him come unto me and drink. He that believeth on me, as the scripture hath said, from within him shall flow rivers of living water. But this spake he of the Spirit, which they that believed on him were to receive: for the Spirit was not yet given; because Jesus was not yet glorified. (John 7.37–39)

At that time the Holy Spirit was not yet given because the Lord Jesus was still to die, be resurrected and ascend back to heaven. The reason the Holy Spirit did not come was not because people did not pray and beg but because the Lord Jesus Christ had not yet been glorified. But when the Lord Jesus *was* glorified, the Holy Spirit did indeed come: "Being therefore by the right hand of God exalted, and having received of the Father the promise of the Holy Spirit, he hath poured forth this, which ye see and hear" (Acts 2.33). The Holy Spirit was poured forth after the Lord Jesus had died, been resurrected and been exalted by God. His descent is therefore due to the Lord himself, and not to our pleading.

In the past we have seen some people begging and penalizing themselves in order to obtain the power of the Holy Spirit. We have also known of other people who thought that those who receive the power of the Holy Spirit must be extraordinary Christians, for surely it is not meant for the ordinary believers. To them, receiving the power of the Holy Spirit is exceptional. Truly, the gift of the Holy Spirit *is* most special and truly the price *is* most expensive, yet it is the Lord Jesus who is the one who has already paid this price. He it is who has died and been raised, therefore we may have the Holy Spirit. The Lord's blood is the cost, the Lord Jesus himself is the source of the Holy Spirit. Naturally, on our side, we need to get rid of all hindrances; otherwise, and no matter how much water there is, it will not be available if the pipe is blocked. If we understand the source of the Holy Spirit and know that Someone else (and not any of us) has already paid the price, do we need to plead piteously for Him?

"Christ redeemed us from the curse of the law, having become a curse for us; for it is written, Cursed is every one that hangeth on a tree: that upon the Gentiles might come the blessing of Abraham in Christ Jesus; that we might receive the promise of the Spirit through faith" (Gal. 3.13,14). We are told here that the purpose of the Lord Jesus' hanging on the cross is for the blessing of Abraham to come upon the Gentiles. What does the blessing of Abraham coming upon the Gentiles mean? It means that by faith we might have the promised Holy Spirit.

If you feel weak, if your spiritual life flows and ebbs intermittently, if you frequently fall and have not the power of the Holy Spirit, you should know that the Lord Jesus has already died and His blood has been shed; therefore, you can come to God and claim the promised Holy Spirit. You may thank God for the blood price already paid by Jesus

Christ, which thus gives you the power of the Holy Spirit. You have no need to live an abnormal life of ups and downs. One thing, however, you must be careful to consider: if any hindrance in your life remains unremoved or if your consecration is less than thorough, you will still not have the power of the Holy Spirit.

We do not plead compellingly for the Holy Spirit. We merely receive what the Lord Jesus has already accomplished. And for this we simply believe and appropriate. For the Bible clearly affirms that since the Lord Jesus has already been sent to fulfill God's will, the Holy Spirit is poured forth upon us.

Question 42

What is the teaching on reconciliation in the Bible? Is it for men to be reconciled to God? or God to be reconciled to men?

Answer:

"All things are of God, who reconciled us to himself through Christ, and gave unto us the ministry of reconciliation; to wit, that God was in Christ reconciling the world unto himself, not reckoning unto them their trespasses, and having committed unto us the word of reconciliation. We are ambassadors therefore on behalf of Christ, as though God were entreating by us: we beseech you on behalf of Christ, be ye reconciled to God" (2 Cor. 5.18–20). These verses show us that the Bible never supports a common misconception of our having to beg God to change His mind in order for us to be saved. God is not One who hates man. For there is no problem on His side. How often we imagine that in view of God's heart being apparently most hard, it takes tens of thousands of pleadings to bend His heart toward pitying and forgiving us. Let it be known that the Bible does not teach this way.

"All things are of God, who reconciled us to himself through Christ"—God reconciled us to himself through Christ. This proves how mistaken it is to fancy that God hates us and that therefore it requires lots of pleadings, confessions, tears, and doing much penance for Him to forgive us. The fact is that God is actually reconciling us to himself through Christ. When Christ was on earth He represented God. Whatever He did for men, each time He did it it stood for how God is. Christ's love toward men manifested God's love in heaven. Then finally, in His death on the cross as the Savior sent by God to be a substitute, we are shown how God reconciled us to himself through Christ. God's heart toward men is peaceful, there is absolutely nothing held against us. So that His treatment of men is totally different from men's thought of Him.

"And gave unto us the ministry of reconciliation": the ministry of the apostles is to persuade men to be reconciled to God. People are thinking how they must entreat Him to pity and to love them, yet they do not realize that He has loved them to the uttermost. How God longs to have them reconciled to himself! Hence in preaching the gospel the apostles beseech men to be reconciled to God; they never ask God to be reconciled to men.

How does God get men to be reconciled to Him? "Not reckoning unto them their trespasses" is the way. God in Christ reconciles the world to himself by His not reckoning unto us our trespasses.

"We are ambassadors therefore on behalf of Christ, as though God was entreating by us: we beseech you on behalf behalf of Christ are entreating that men be reconciled to God; they do not ask God to be reconciled to them. People may think God does not want to be reconciled to them, but in actuality He has entrusted to the apostles the task of entreating them to be reconciled to Him. The command we receive from God is to beseech people, on His behalf, to be reconciled to Him; it is not an asking God to be reconciled to them. So no one needs to plead piteously with Him; he only needs to believe and to accept what Christ has accomplished.

Yet does not God hate sin, you may ask? No doubt God does hate sin. But if anyone receives the Lord Jesus Christ, his sins are forgiven him by God. We should therefore be very careful lest we give people a wrong impression that God's heart is one of hatred toward *them*.

Question 43

What is the condition for salvation (that is, for receiving eternal life)?

Answer:

According to the Bible, there is but one condition to our being saved, and that is, to believe. There is absolutely no need to add anything to faith. Unfortunately many consider faith as not enough, and so they always want to add on something extra in order to be saved. This is due to their not understanding what it is we believe, what faith actually is, what is the effect of faith, and how living faith is expressed. Anyone who truly believes is saved; there is no need to add any other condition. Let us now review seven items which are not conditions at all of salvation.

(a) *Not faith plus hope.* Some think that to be saved one must believe and then pray earnestly, hoping God will be merciful to him and get him to heaven. Yet the Bible does not say we should expect God to show mercy, we should instead believe that He has *already* shown mercy. "But now apart from the law a righteousness of God has been manifested, being witnessed by the law and the prophets; even the righteousness of God through faith in Jesus Christ unto all them that believe; for there is no distinction" (Rom. 3.21,22). For that person who accounts himself as one who believes and yet is one who is still hoping, his faith is undependable and not real. For faith is a believing that it already has been done. Such a person therefore does not know what faith is, neither does he understand the heart of God. He regards God as most reluctant to forgive, so he must plead till He has mercy on him. Do you know that God has already forgiven you? In shedding His precious blood the Lord Jesus is forgiving all your sins. This fact is already established. By believing, you will receive forgiveness. If you believe, the forgiveness which the Lord has accomplished is yours. If you believe that Jesus Christ has died for you, the grace of God shall be manifested in you.

(b) *Not faith plus confession.* Some say if a person believes and yet does not confess Christ, he cannot be saved. Doubtless the one who believes must confess Christ. But he is not saved because of his confession, since confession is not a condition for salvation.

"Every one therefore who shall confess me before men,

him will I also confess before my Father who is in heaven. But whosoever shall deny me before men, him will I also deny before my Father who is in heaven" (Matt. 10.32,33). This passage does not apply to our receiving eternal life. On the contrary, it points to a person's place in the kingdom of the heavens to come. It refers to the salvation of the believer's soul by indicating that if anyone is willing to deny himself and confess the Lord on earth today he shall be acknowledged by the Lord before the Father in the future. It does not speak of eternal salvation.

"Whosoever shall be ashamed of me and of my words in this adulterous and sinful generation, the Son of man also shall be ashamed of him, when he cometh in the glory of his Father with the holy angels" (Mark 8.38). This too refers to the kingdom time. Earlier in Mark it is mentioned that "whosoever would save his life shall lose it; and whosoever shall lose his life for my sake and the gospel's shall save it" (8.35). "Life" in the Greek original is "soul". What is meant by losing his soul on earth? It means forfeiting while on earth all the enjoyments within the soul for the sake of the Lord. He who is afraid of losing his face or is ashamed of the Lord today will certainly lose his face and be put to shame in the future. Anyone who is not afraid to lose face today for the sake of the Lord or who is not ashamed of the Lord shall definitely receive glory in the future. Whoever is unwilling to suffer with the Lord now shall not gain the glory of the kingdom then. How very many will miss the glory when the Lord Jesus Christ sets up His kingdom on earth!

Both Matthew 10.32,33 and Mark 8.35,38 therefore speak of the kingdom, not of eternal life. Entry into the kingdom is directly related to the believer's conduct on earth. If a believer does not confess the Lord as he should, he will have no part in the kingdom, even though he has eternal life.

"With the heart man believeth unto righteousness; and with the mouth confession is made unto salvation" (Rom. 10.10). It is clearly stated here that with the mouth confession is made to salvation. But to understand what this means we must look into the context. The theme of Romans 10 is the righteousness which is by faith. "Christ is the end of the law unto righteousness to every one that believeth" (v.4). Faith is the condition for having righteousness. Now what about this faith? "The word is nigh thee, in thy mouth, and in thy heart: . . . because if thou shalt confess with thy mouth Jesus as Lord, and shalt believe in thy heart that God raised him from the dead, thou shalt be saved" (vv.8,9).

Hence faith here includes two sides: one side is done by the mouth and the other side is done by the heart. Both are the actions of faith, being the two sides of one thing—just as justification and salvation are but two sides of the same thing. To confess with the mouth is an expression of faith and is therefore included in faith. And that is why in the concluding remark only faith is mentioned, and not confession as well: "Whosoever believeth on him shall not be put to shame" (v.11). It does not say that whosoever believes on Him and confesses Him shall not be put to shame. "How then shall they call on him in whom they have not believed?" (v.14); "Who hath believed our report?" (v.16); "So belief cometh of hearing" (v.17)—in none of these places is confession mentioned. Hence confession does not stand alone by itself, it is only the natural expression of faith. What, then, is the confession mentioned here? It does not refer to our standing up and testifying, rather is it like the crying aloud of "Mama!" when a child recognizes its mother. Even so, as soon as a person believes in his heart, his mouth will most naturally cry out with "Abba, Father" (Rom. 8.15; Gal. 4.6). Accordingly, confession is not another additional condition for salvation. Only believe and you shall be saved.

(c) *Not faith plus good works.* Some may feel that, being a sinner, he ought to have good works. It is too cheap a thing to be saved simply by believing in Jesus; he should do good as well as believe in Jesus; only in this way shall his salvation be guaranteed. But this is not the teaching of the Bible. Unquestionably, the aim in God saving us is to have us to do good subsequently; for is it not stated that "we are . . . created in Christ Jesus for good works" and that we are "prepared unto every good work" (Eph. 2.10; 2 Tim. 2.21)? Do let us remember that what the Bible tells us is that good works *follow* salvation. It is not good works toward salvation, nor is it that faith *plus* good works is salvation. Do consider the fact that a little child is not able to walk before he is even born. In like manner, we must be born again before we can do good. If anyone expects to do good before he is even born, he should be shown plainly that no such possibility exists anywhere in the entire world.

"Now to him that worketh, the reward is not reckoned as of grace, but as of debt. But to him that worketh not, but believeth on him that justifieth the ungodly, his faith is reckoned for righteousness. Even as David also pronounceth blessing upon the man, unto whom God reckoneth righteousness apart from works" (Rom. 4.4-6). He who works earns the wages; his wages cannot be reckoned as grace but as his due. But he who does not work and yet believes—let us underline the word "believeth"—in God who justifies the sinner, has his faith reckoned to him for righteousness. Here it is no work, only faith—not faith plus something else. Keep well in mind that faith alone is sufficient. Hence David pronounces blessing upon the man whom God reckons as being righteous apart from works.

"By grace have ye been saved through faith; and that not of yourselves, it is the gift of God; not of works, that no man should glory. For we are his workmanship, created in Christ Jesus for good works, which God afore prepared that we should walk in them" (Eph. 2.8–10). Verses 8 and 9 tell us that we are saved by grace and through the faith which God has given us, not at all by our own works. Then verse 10 tells us that God has saved us in order that we may do the good works which He has prepared for us beforehand. So we are saved by grace through faith; and after being saved we should do the good works which God has earlier prepared for us.

(d) *Not faith plus prayer.* Some may view prayer as a condition for salvation, not knowing that we are saved by faith and not by prayer. Since the Lord Jesus Christ has already borne our sins and was judged by God, all we need to do is to believe; we do not even need to pray. Prayer is asking God to do it, but faith is believing He has already done it. We are to believe that God has judged Jesus Christ who died in our stead. The cross has already completed the work of redemption, so that whoever believes in what God has done shall be saved.

Someone may raise the question, Does it not say in Romans 10.13 that "whosoever shall call upon the name of the Lord shall be saved"? Does this not then imply that no one can be saved without prayer? Yet we find this verse is immediately followed by another which declares: "How then shall they call on him in whom they have not believed?" (v.14a) The correct order is: first believe, then call. Call after there is faith. Hence calling is an expression of our believing; it is not an independent and additional condition. Faith includes asking, faith spontaneously leads to asking. Moreover, the asking here is not in the sense of

ordinary prayer, it is rather a calling upon the name of the
Lord. It is the same as "confess with thy mouth Jesus as
Lord" in the passage preceding it. It is similar to the calling
on the name of the Lord as described in 1 Corinthians 12:
"No man can say, Jesus is Lord, but in the Holy Spirit"
(v.3). The name of the Lord is salvation to us. Whoever
calls on His name, that is, saying Jesus is Lord, shall be
saved. How can anyone say Jesus is Lord if he does not
already believe that Jesus is indeed Lord? How can anyone
believe that Jesus is Lord and fail to call upon His name?
So prayer is not a condition for salvation, faith alone is.

(e) *Not faith plus baptism.* Now someone may suggest that
even though salvation does not depend on hope, confession,
works, or prayer, nevertheless only he who believes and is
baptized is saved. Such a concept is also incorrect. Yes,
Mark 16.16 does in fact state that "he that believeth and is
baptized shall be saved", but we should notice what the
word "saved" points to. The Bible mentions several kinds of
salvation such as eternal salvation, believer's daily salvation, saved from affliction and physical deliverance, and
salvation of the soul. The salvation which is related to
baptism refers especially to being saved from this sinful
world. This is different from having eternal life. Having
eternal life is a personal acceptance of life eternal, but
baptism is to be saved out of the evil system of the world.
One who believes and yet is not baptized has eternal life in
him, but he will still be viewed by the world as an unsaved
person. He must rise up and be baptized—declaring thereby
that he has severed his relation with the evil world—before
he will be acknowledged by the people that he is a saved
person.

As to having eternal life—that is, coming out of
judgment and being eternally saved—all he needs is faith

and nothing else. For we must note that the second part of Mark 16.16 continues with: "but he that disbelieveth shall be condemned"; it does not say, He that disbelieves and is not baptized shall be condemned. On the other hand, to be saved from the evil system of this world does require faith and baptism, whereas unbelief alone is enough for condemnation. In other words, the condition for not being condemned is simply "believe", not "believe and be baptized". The malefactor on the cross was not baptized, yet the Lord said to him: "Today shalt thou be with me in Paradise" (Luke 23.40–44). He had believed, so he was not condemned. He was saved and received eternal life. Consequently, baptism is not a condition for eternal life.

(f) *Not faith plus confession of sin.* Someone may fancy that his sins are as scrolls hanging on the cross. Each time he confesses his sin a scroll is taken down; and whatever sin is unconfessed remains hanging there. The Bible never teaches such a way. This does not mean, of course, that we do not need to confess our sins. Quite the contrary, Christians ought to confess. Yet confession of sin is not a condition for salvation.

But does not 1 John 1.9 say: "If we confess our sins, he is faithful and righteous to forgive us our sins, and to cleanse us from all unrighteousness"? Does not this tell us that we should confess our sins? It is true that there is such a verse in the Bible; even so, let us be clear that 1 John is not written to unbelievers. The "we" here refers to Christians because this letter is written to believers. Now in this letter, three classes of Christians are continually being mentioned: (1) little children who have life, (2) young men who have power, and (3) fathers who have experience. 1 John speaks of fellowship. If a Christian sins, he must confess his sin; otherwise, his fellowship with God will be hindered. In order to have his fellowship with God restored he must confess his sin.

It is very wrong, though, to tell an unbeliever that he needs to confess his sins in order to be saved. As a sinner is being convicted by the Holy Spirit of sin, of righteousness, and of judgment, he believes in the finished work of the Son of God and his sins are all forgiven before God. The condition for a sinner to be forgiven by God is faith. Nowhere in the whole Bible can it be found that for a sinner to be saved he must believe plus confess his sins. Jesus Christ has already accomplished the work of redemption; and whoever believes in the witness which God renders concerning His Son shall be saved.

(g) *Not faith plus repentance.* Quite a few maintain that salvation depends on repentance. The book of Romans presents most clearly the salvation of God, yet not once does it ever mention salvation by works. The Gospel according to John expresses itself most definitely on the gospel, but it never once says that salvation is through repentance. Salvation hinges on faith, not on repentance.

Does this mean that repentance is unnecessary? According to the Scriptures, those who believe must first repent; but even believers must also repent. Before the exercise of initial faith there is repentance; and after once believing, there is also the necessity of repentance. Unless a person changes his views on sin, on himself, on the world, and on the Lord, it is not possible for him to be saved. The very meaning of the term "repentance" signifies a change of mind. What one considers as precious before salvation is now looked upon as dross. Repentance is therefore not a condition for salvation; it is instead an element attached to faith and thus to salvation.

What is faith? Faith is not believing in some theological doctrines. We do hear the doctrines, but we believe in Christ. "In whom ye also, having heard the word of the truth, the gospel of your salvation,—in whom, having also believed, ye were sealed with the Holy Spirit of promise" (Eph. 1.13). Hearing is hearing the word, a hearing the gospel; but believing is a believing in Christ. Some acknowledge that they have believed, yet actually they may only be agreeing to certain doctrines—they may not have believed in Christ. Or, some people may profess to believe for some ulterior reason, but they never really know Christ. Such persons are not saved. Hence preaching of doctrines can never serve as our aim; our aim is for people to believe in Christ.

What is meant by believing in Christ? Consider what 1 John 5 tells us:

> If we receive the witness of men, the witness of God is greater: for the witness of God is this, that he hath borne witness concerning his Son. He that believeth on the Son of God hath the witness in him: he that believeth not God hath made him a liar; because he hath not believed in the witness that God hath borne concerning his Son. And the witness is this, that God gave unto us eternal life, and this life is in his Son. He that hath the Son hath the life; he that hath not the Son of God hath not the life. (vv.9–12)

Faith is none other than receiving the witness which God has borne regarding His Son. Whoever believes in the Son of God has eternal life.

We rejoice today because we are saved by faith and not by any other requirement. We should have good works, we should confess Christ before men, we should repent and confess our sins, we should also be baptized and pray much—so that God may be pleased with us. But we do not depend on these things to get saved. We are saved through faith alone.

Question 44

What is the unpardonable sin? Is it that whoever commits this sin cannot be saved? What is the meaning of this sin?

Answer:

The unpardonable sin is that of blaspheming the Holy Spirit. Wherever the Holy Spirit works, the devil is also at work; he is never lazy. Sometimes the devil will stretch the truth of the Bible a little further so as to torment people. When the Holy Spirit is convicting a person of his sins, the devil will tell the man:—You are a sinner, a chief sinner, a special sinner who has committed the sin of blaspheming the Holy Spirit; therefore, you will never be forgiven. Many people are in fear lest they have committed the sin of blaspheming the Holy Spirit. So let us first explain the meaning of this sin, and then we can draw the conclusion which we come to that no one today is able to commit this sin. Let us read Mark 3.28–30.

"Verily I say unto you, all their sins shall be forgiven unto the sons of men, and their blasphemies wherewith soever they shall blaspheme" (v.28). This sounds like music! It is a most pleasant word! All the sins and blasphemies of the world may be forgiven. What a great declaration of the gospel! All sins include great sins, small sins, refined sins, gross sins, sins which are humanly considered as unpardonable as well as those that are viewed as pardonable, and sins of yesterday, today, and even tomorrow. Hallelujah! All sins are forgiven! Words of blasphemy against God are forgiven, slanders against the Lord are also forgiven. All sins—that is, all our actions of conduct and all our words spoken against God while we were yet sinners—are all forgiven. There is not any sin that cannot be forgiven, even every blasphemous word against God is forgiven. This is what the Lord says here.

Do not imagine that you have committed the unpardonable sin. Words spoken against God and against Christ are not to be considered as blasphemy against the Holy Spirit. The only unpardonable sin is blasphemy against the Holy Spirit, not against Christ. Quenching the Holy Spirit is not the same as blaspheming against Him, nor is resisting the Holy Spirit a blaspheming against Him.

"But whosoever shall blaspheme against the Holy Spirit hath never forgiveness, but is guilty of an eternal sin" (v.29). It is therefore evident that this sin is a special and unordinary kind.

What is blasphemy against the Holy Spirit? It is to speak out openly words which blaspheme the Holy Spirit. How do we know that this sin is spoken out of the mouth? Please read the concluding verse which says: "Because they said, He hath an unclean spirit" (v.30). Hence this sin is not so easily committed as many today think. To commit such a sin a person must clearly witness the Lord casting out demons and performing miracles and wonders while He was on earth, and in spite of his knowledge of all these things he still insists that the Lord has an unclean spirit.

Because of all this, therefore, for people to commit this sin they must (1) see the Lord Jesus with their eyes, (2) witness the Lord doing wonders in their midst, (3) know assuredly that this is of the Holy Spirit, and (4) in the face of such inner conviction speak nevertheless that this is the work of the demons. How, then, can we today commit this sin of blasphemy against the Holy Spirit if we have not seen the Lord with our eyes, neither have witnessed Him doing wonders in our midst, nor have known definitely that this is of the Holy Spirit? Hence we may conclude that we do not have the opportunity nor the possibility of committing such a sin. In case anybody or even the devil should say to you that you are never to be forgiven because you have committed the sin of blasphemy against the Holy Spirit, you may answer at once that there is no such thing because you have not seen the Lord nor His wonders, neither have you spoken willfully that the work is done by demons while knowing assuredly it is of the Holy Spirit.

Once a newly saved brother asked an elderly brother, "Have I committed the sin of blasphemy against the Holy Spirit?" The answer to him was excellent. "If you are still able to grieve for your sins," he replied, "then this is a proof that you have not committed the sin of blasphemy against the Holy Spirit." This answer is full of truth. We may add one more word by saying that even concerning one who is not conscious of his sins, he too may not be described as having committed the sin of blasphemy against the Holy Spirit.

Let us see how Matthew records the discussion of this matter: "Whosoever shall speak a word against the Son of man, it shall be forgiven him; but whosoever shall speak against the Holy Spirit, it shall not be forgiven him, neither in this world, nor in that which is to come" (12.32). These are words spoken by the Lord Jesus to the Jews, who did commit the sin as recorded in this chapter. They clearly saw how the Lord had cast out demons by the Holy Spirit, and yet they stubbornly maintained that He had cast these demons out by Beelzebub the prince of the demons. How does the Bible describe these Jews? "Unto them is fulfilled the prophecy of Isaiah, which saith, By hearing ye shall hear, and shall in no wise understand; and seeing ye shall see, and shall in no wise perceive: for this people's heart is waxed gross, and their ears are dull of hearing, and their eyes they have closed" (Matt. 13.14,15a). Thus are we shown that if a person has committed the sin of blasphemy against the Holy Spirit, he will in no wise be sensitive to sin; nor shall he be saved, because his heart has waxed gross, his ears are dull of hearing, and his eyes are closed.

There are words in two other Scripture passages which are very meaningful to this subject. One passage is found in Luke 8: "And those by the wayside are they that have heard; then cometh the devil, and taketh away the word from their heart, that they may not believe and be saved" (v.12). Not only the Lord but the devil too knows that as soon as a man believes, he is saved; and hence he is fearful lest any man believes and is saved. The other passage is found in Matthew 13: "He answered and said unto them, Unto you it is given to know the mysteries of the kingdom of heaven, but to them it is not given . . . Therefore speak I to them in parables; . . . lest haply they should perceive with their eyes, and hear with their ears, and understand with their heart, and should turn again, and I should heal them" (v.11–15). Concerning those who have blasphemed against the Holy Spirit, God is fearful that they might come to be saved. For this reason, the Lord speaks in parables lest they should indeed turn again and be healed. Hallelujah! How wonderful is the word "believe and be saved".

Whoever shall blaspheme against the Holy Spirit shall never be forgiven, for he "is guilty of an eternal sin" (Mark 3.29). According to the opinion of some Bible scholars, this can also be translated as: he "is in the grasp of an everlasting trespass". Yet someone may ask why it says he cannot be forgiven in this age or the age to come (Matt. 12.32). Simply because he will sin forever. But how can he sin in hell, for what torments him most in hell are worms and fire. We must see that in hell there is not only the suffering because of a lack of water even insufficient to wet the fingertip so as to cool the tongue, but there is also the burning of the fire of lusts. Hell is where sin and lusts are never satisfied. It is a most miserable place. But we may thank and praise God that if only we are willing to believe, there is no sin that can block us from being saved. For the Lord himself says: "All their sins shall be forgiven unto the sons of men, and their blasphemies wherewith soever they shall blaspheme" (Mark 3.28). Consequently, we may be at peace.

Although we today will not be able to commit the sin of blasphemy against the Holy Spirit, we should nonetheless be very careful in saying so-and-so's work is of the Holy Spirit whereas so-and-so's work is of the evil spirit.

Question 45

What is meant by having "fallen away from grace" (Gal. 5.4)? Will a person who has fallen away from grace be saved?

Answer:

There are several books in the New Testament which bear a close resemblance to each other in reading them— books such as Ephesians and Colossians, Galatians and Romans. Why do they have such a resemblance? Because one makes a positive statement while the other discusses the matter in a negative way or in opposite terms. Ephesians tells us that the church is the body of Christ, but Colossians turns around and says that Christ is the head of the church. Romans presents from the positive side that justification is by God's grace, based on God's righteousness, and obtained by man's faith; Galatians proceeds from the negative side to say that no one is justified by works nor saved by the law. Romans advances what the truth is, whereas Galatians declares what is not the truth. By knowing what is not the truth, the knowledge of the truth is increased.

The believers in Galatia had a good beginning, for they were clearly saved through faith. There then developed a danger among them because some people maintained that though the beginning of salvation did come through faith in Christ, the operation of the Holy Spirit, and the grace of God, yet once having been saved, people must keep the law of God and try their best to do good if they would merit God's pleasure. If you were to ask someone how he was saved, he would answer, By faith. But if you were then to ask him how he could obtain God's pleasure, he would say, By doing good. This is precisely the condition of the Galatian believers. They knew they were saved by faith but they must now maintain this salvation by keeping the law: first they must be circumcised, and next they must observe the many ordinances of the Old Testament. In view of all this Paul had to reprimand these people by saying: "Ye are severed from Christ, ye who would be justified by the law; ye are fallen away from grace" (5.4).

What does "fallen away from grace" mean? From Galatians 5.1 we know that these people had already entered into grace. "For freedom did Christ set us free: stand fast therefore, and be not entangled again in a yoke of bondage." Christ had set them free; therefore they should now stand in this freedom and not be entangled again in the yoke of bondage. So what is meant by "fallen away from grace"? Well, if one moves away from the place of freedom in which he originally stood, he makes for himself a yoke to bear. This is viewed as a having "fallen away from grace". Yet this basically has nothing to do with whether or not one can be saved. Quite the opposite, only he who has already been saved is able to fall away from grace.

Every Christian obtains a new position on the day he is saved. He also has obtained a liberty which is his as a child of God. Liberty is not licentiousness. It is having a free spirit to come before God. We are not required to do hard labor, neither keep the days, nor to be circumcised.

What is the difference before God between a Christian who is not free and one who is free? When a Christian who is free comes to God, all he remembers is that he is accepted by Him through the Lord Jesus. He forgets himself, not even does he look into himself; for he knows that he has boldness to enter the holy place by the blood of Jesus. However, a Christian who is not free will be most wary from morning till night. If during the day he treats people well, reads the Bible with joy, and prays at some length, he will seem to become bolder when he attends the church meeting, and his amens will be uttered more loudly than usual. But if on a particular day he has not done too well, he will imagine that God is displeased with him. Such kind of Christian always turns his eyes inward, thus forgetting to see what Christ has already accomplished. He surmises that God will be pleased with him if he does well, but that God will be displeased with him if he does not do so well. From dawn to dusk he is fashioning an iron yoke for himself, a yoke composed of the strictest laws for himself to keep.

We should realize that the freedom which Paul talks about refers not to position, nor to salvation, but to the

Christian's daily enjoyment of that freedom in grace which God has given us. Such freedom is not licentiousness, not an unrestricted permissiveness to do anything one wishes. This freedom is a freedom before God, given to us through Jesus Christ. If a person comes before God and forgets the blood and looks at himself he is committing a great sin, because he has neglected the blood which God highly values. Hebrews 10.29 tells us that whoever counts the blood of the covenant an unholy thing commits a grave sin. The blood is so valuable in God's sight that the Bible calls it "precious blood". Anyone who fails to look at the precious blood before God will lose the enjoyment of grace in this life.

"Ye are severed from Christ" in Galatians 5.4 means not having the blessings of this life. If one is saved, he naturally will have the blessings of after life; but if he does not know how to live daily by that which Christ has accomplished, he is not able to enjoy the blessings which Christ gives to him day by day. A shackled Christian makes a yoke for himself to bear; he lives as a slave, not as a freeman before God.

The Bible places a great emphasis on the work of Christ. It tells us that God accepts us because of the work of Christ, not because of our own works. Each time we come to God it is based on what Christ is before God, not on what we are before Him. For He esteems *Christ* highly and not us. Even if one should act better than Peter, John and Paul, he still comes to God through Christ. It is Christ who brings a person to God, not his own good works.

Yet having said that we come to God by what Christ has accomplished, we need to say something about our coming before men. For can we say that since our coming to God is through what Christ has accomplished we need not have good works before men? Let it be understood that our light should shine before men. Let our light shine before them that they may see our good works and glorify our Father who is in heaven (Matt. 5.16). If our conduct is bad, who in the world will acknowledge us as Christians?

The position which Christ has given us before God is most secure. Each day each time we come to God we ought to come with a conscience void of offense. Nevertheless, some Christians always feel guilty as they come before Him. But has not Hebrews 10.2 declared that "the worshippers, having been once cleansed, would have had no more consciousness of sins"? With our conscience once cleansed by the blood, we are forever free before God.

Question 46

Will the class of people mentioned in Hebrews 6.4–8 perish?

Answer:

Let us read from verse 1 to verse 8 of Hebrews 6:

Wherefore leaving the doctrine of the first principles of Christ, let us press on unto perfection; not laying again a foundation of repentance from dead works, and of faith toward God, of the teaching of baptisms, and of laying on of hands, and of resurrection of the dead, and of eternal judgment. And this will we do, if God permit. For as touching those who were once enlightened and tasted of the heavenly gift, and were made partakers of the Holy Spirit, and tasted the good word of God, and the powers of the age to come, *and then fell away, it is impossible to renew them again unto repentance; seeing they crucify to themselves the Son of God afresh, and put him to an open shame.* For the land which hath drunk

the rain that cometh oft upon it, and bringeth forth herbs
meet for them for whose sake it is also tilled, receiveth
blessing from God: *but if it beareth thorns and thistles, it is rejected
and nigh unto a curse; whose end is to be burned.*

Some people after reading verses 6 and 8 (italicized
above) conclude that this class of people cannot be saved.
Who are they? According to verses 4 and 5 they are people
who fall away from the truth after they have experienced
four things: (1) have once been enlightened, (2) have tasted
of the heavenly gift, (3) have been made partakers of the
Holy Spirit, and (4) have tasted the good word of God and
the powers of the age to come. Their consequence will be:
are "rejected and nigh unto a curse, whose end is to be
burned" (v.8). Basing their conclusion on this last verse,
some judge that this class of people is not saved. If such is
really the case, then a person who has eternal life is able to
lose it—which is to say, that he who is saved may be
"unsaved". How can we explain it?

Let us first understand what the book of Hebrews is
talking about. Hebrews speaks about "pressing on"; and
our progress of pressing onward is twofold: (1) Christians
must grow, and (2) those who teach others must grow too.
Christians should know the Lord progressively more in their
lives; those who teach others should also teach more
advanced truth; that is, they should not only teach on
salvation from the beginning to the end of the year, they
should teach even deeper truth.

The peak concerning progress spoken in Hebrews is
reached in Chapters 5 and 6. Chapter 5 speaks of Melchizedek, about whom the writer says: "Of whom we have
many things to say, and hard of interpretation, seeing ye
are become dull of hearing" (v.11). You ought to have fully
grown, yet you are still pitifully old babies. You should be

able to take the solid food of the word of righteousness but, sad to say, you are in need of milk. Then Chapter 6 is addressed to those who teach. In their teaching there should be progress instead of confining it merely to the six elementary doctrines of repentance from dead works, faith toward God, the teaching of baptisms, the laying on of hands, resurrection of the dead, and eternal judgment. So we may plainly perceive that Hebrews 6.1–8 does not deal with the problem of initial salvation but with the problem of progress. The aim of this Epistle to the Hebrews is to point toward progress, not toward salvation. We will be seriously mistaken if we confuse the theme.

A number of Christians pay no attention to the truth of the church or the truth of the kingdom; their eyes are exclusively fixed on salvation as if that is all. But the Bible is not totally devoted to the matter of salvation; it tells us of many other things.

Hence let us first lay hold of the theme of the epistle before we look into this particular portion of Hebrews. Now the passage before us may be divided into three sections: (a) verses 1–3, "not again"; (b) verses 4–6, "impossible"; (c) verses 7 and 8, which can be entitled "should not". Let us take up each in order.

(a) *Not again.* "Not again" is in reference to six things; namely, repentance from dead works, faith toward God, teaching of baptisms, laying on of hands, resurrection of the dead, and eternal judgment. We are told about "not laying again a foundation". These six items are foundational truths. Since the foundation is already laid, it need not be laid again. Who will ever build a house by laying the foundation all the time? After the foundation is laid, the work should proceed onward.

(b) *Impossible*. "Once" in verse 4 refers back to a historical fact. "Again" in verse 6 is the same word as the "again" in verse 1. The coordinate conjunction "and" in this section joins four things together; namely, once enlightened, tasted of the heavenly gift, made partakers of the Holy Spirit, and tasted the good word of God and the powers of the age to come. Hence what is said here is, that if a person already has experienced these four things it is impossible for him to be renewed again unto repentance if he falls away. For this person has only fallen—he has not forsaken the course he runs. Since his direction is still correct, how can he ever renew his repentance, crucify again the Son of God, and put Him to an open shame?

The writer of this letter told the Hebrews in verses 1–3 that they had no need of laying again the foundation. Some might retort: But what if a person fits the description in verses 4–6? Must he not lay the foundation again if he falls away? Should he not be renewed again to repentance? The answer of the writer was: Even though one may have the conditions of verses 4–6, that is to say, a situation in which he has really sinned, it is still impossible for him to be renewed to repentance.

Can we be born again and then be unborn? Can we be renewed to repentance and be reborn? The repentance in verse 6 is the same repentance as in verse 1, so it is repentance as a foundation. This does not suggest that one should not repent again; it only affirms that no one could go back to the foundational position and renew himself to repentance. That, then, is the big difference. Take special note of the word "again"—renew again to repentance, laying again a foundation of repentance. Not again, because it is impossible.

Therefore, this passage does not instruct us that if a person falls after he has received so much spiritual benefits he must renew his original repentance and lay again the foundation. Regeneration happens only once. Who will start all over again if he merely falls on the way? Even so, many people entertain such a misconception as this.

(c) *Should not.* Although verses 1–3 tell us "not again" and verses 4–6 tell us "impossible", verses 7 and 8 tell us that we "should not", which means that we should not continue to fall, we should not always sin, lest we seem to crucify the Son of God afresh and put Him to an open shame. We will be disciplined if we really do so. Hence we should not do it.

Some people assume that if a person sins after he is saved he will be unsaved. Other people believe that after one is saved he will not be punished regardless of what sin he commits. Both of these views are incorrect. God expects a saved person to grow and to make progress. Just as no one can go back to his mother's womb and be born again after he has lived a bad life for several decades, so spiritually he cannot go back to lay again the foundation if he ever falls away. But what if he really continues doing bad things? There will be three consequences; namely, (1) rejected, (2) brought nigh to a curse, and (3) be burned.

(1) Rejected—This is the same word as the "rejected" found in 1 Corinthians 9.27. There Paul describes how he buffets his body and brings it into bondage lest by any means after he has preached to others he himself should be rejected. Naturally every Christian knows that Paul is not in danger of becoming unsaved, but that he is afraid lest he miss the crown and the kingdom.

What is meant by being rejected of God? For example, you have a bicycle which was originally in good shape and fit to be used, but now it is broken and rusted and cannot be used. By saying this it does not mean that this bicycle has disappeared; it is only being rejected, put aside because useless. To be rejected by God does not mean that a person has lost eternal life or is unsaved; it only means he is set aside by God and has thus become useless. To those believers who continue in sins, God has His discipline of putting them outside of glory—in outer darkness—without any part in the kingdom. This is what Matthew 25.30 means.

(2) *Brought nigh to a curse*—Here it says *nigh* to a curse, not a curse itself. Nigh to a curse looks like a curse, and yet it is not to be cursed. What is being stressed here is not so much a matter of the degree of punishment as it is the fact of punishment itself. Not only unbelievers will be punished, Christians too will be punished. Therefore it says nigh to a curse.

Let us be very careful lest we deign to think that no matter what a Christian does he will not be punished. Remember that "nigh unto a curse" implies there is punishment.

(3) *Be burned*—This fits in well with what 1 Corinthians 3.15 says about God's fire burning up the person's work. Such a person is like a living garbage can in which are stored many unclean things that will be purified through the fire.

We should rejoice on the one hand and be warned on the other. Our salvation is safe and secure on the one side, yet on the other side we will receive punishment if we do not behave. Although such punishment is not permanent, we shall have no part in the millennial kingdom.

To sum up, then, Hebrews 6.1-3 states that the foundation is not to be laid again; verses 4-6 explain that it is impossible to again lay the foundation from whence a believer has fallen but there must be a rising up, since there is no possibility of going back to renew his first repentance;

and verses 7 and 8 conclude that one should not misbehave, because he will surely be punished if he persists.

Question 47

What is meant by "there remaineth no more a sacrifice for sins" (Heb. 10.26)?

Answer:

"If we sin wilfully after that we have received the knowledge of the truth, there remaineth no more a sacrifice for sins" (Heb. 10.26). What is meant by "no more a sacrifice for sins"? Some people will say: "If I sin willfully after I have known the truth, I will not be saved. It is true that God has caused His Son to bear my sins and die for me that I might be saved through believing in His Son; but if I sin willfully, then according to Hebrews 10.26 there does not remain anymore sacrifice for sins, and consequently I will not be saved. Furthermore, the next verse states that there remains 'a certain fearful expectation of judgment, and a fierceness of fire which shall devour the adversaries' (v.27). So if I sin willfully, I can only wait for two things: one is judgment, the other is the fire which shall devour the adversaries, which is hell or perdition." In the view of these people this passage of the Scriptures is directed at Christians; so that if a Christian sins willfully he cannot be saved. Let us now see whether "if we sin wilfully" has reference to Christians or to another class of people. We shall also want to see if "sin wilfully" points to ordinary sin or rather to some specific sin.

According to the statement of the Bible, those people who "sin wilfully after that [they] have received the knowledge of the truth" have "a certain fearful expectation of judgment, and a fierceness of fire which shall devour the adversaries". Therefore, these cannot be that class of persons, mentioned in Hebrews 6, "who were once enlightened and tasted of the heavenly gift". The "truth" mentioned here is that truth spoken of in the first part of Hebrews 10, which is the redemption accomplished once and for all by the Lord Jesus Christ. Such people know of the death of the Lord Jesus, of His shed blood and broken body. They even know that they can enter the holy place boldly through the blood of the Lord Jesus and be accepted by God, and that the sacrifice for sins has been offered once and for all, so that the work of redemption is forever completed. Now if these people should sin willfully after they have had such knowledge of the truth as this, then there remains no more a sacrifice for sins.

We need to see that if the above verses could be applied to a Christian, that is, if a Christian is tempted to lie and steal, to frequent places he ought not to go, or do things he knows he should not do, and is thereby considered as sinning willfully and is therefore not saved, *who* then shall be saved? Even Paul and Peter would probably not qualify for being saved! Has not Paul the believer confessed: "For not what I would, that do I practise; but what I hate, that I do. . . . For the good which I would I do not: but the evil which I would not, that I practise. . . . Wretched man that I am! who shall deliver me out of the body of this death?" (Rom. 7.15,19,24) Does not Paul practice the evil he knows he should not do and does not do the good he knows he should do? And has not the believing Peter denied the Lord thrice before a maid? Does he not know that he is lying and that lying is sin? From all this we can know that the phrase "sin wilfully" must mean something special and not just committing a sin that one knows.

Yet this can be proven even in another way. To do so, we need to read the text of this Scripture passage all in one breath from verse 26 through 29:

> For if we sin wilfully after that we have received the knowledge of the truth, there remaineth no more a sacrifice for sins, but a certain fearful expectation of judgment, and a fierceness of fire which shall devour the adversaries. A man that hath set at nought Moses' law dieth without compassion on the word of two or three witnesses: of how much sorer punishment, think ye, shall he be judged worthy, who hath trodden under foot the Son of God, and hath counted the blood of the covenant wherewith he was sanctified an unholy thing, and hath done despite unto the Spirit of grace?

What is really meant by "sin wilfully" in verse 26? It points to the three things in verse 29; namely, (1) trodden underfoot the Son of God, (2) counted the blood of the covenant wherewith he was sanctified as an unholy thing, and (3) done despite to the Spirit of grace. In sum, it means to reject the gospel of salvation. He has heard the word of God which states that Jesus is the Son of God, yet he answers by saying that Jesus is a bastard. He has heard God's word which says that Jesus has shed His blood for the remission of sins and that His blood is most precious—even as the blood of a pure spotless lamb, but he replies by saying that the death of Jesus is a martyr's death and that the blood Jesus shed is common just like anybody else's. He has heard the word of God which says that the Holy Spirit brings repentance and gives eternal life, nevertheless he retorts by declaring that he does not believe God will impart to him what Jesus has accomplished nor that he believes in new birth. Because of this kind of reaction, the

Bible's word is that there remains to him no more sacrifice for sins.

What is meant by "there remaineth no more a sacrifice for sins"? "No more" indicates that there once was. We must pay particular attention to this word "more". In this connection please note the following passages of the Scriptures:

"Who needeth not daily, like those high priests, to offer up sacrifices, first for his own sins, and then for the sins of the people: for this he did *once* for all, when he offered up himself" (Heb. 7.27).

"Nor yet through the blood of goats and calves, but through his own blood, entered in *once* for all into the holy place, having obtained eternal redemption" (Heb. 9.12).

"Nor yet that he should offer himself *often*, as the high priest entereth into the holy place year by year with blood not his own; else must he *often* have suffered since the foundation of the world: but now *once* at the end of the ages hath he been manifested to put away sin by the sacrifice of himself. . . . So Christ also, having been *once* offered to bear the sins of many . . ." (Heb. 9.25–28).

"Else would they not have ceased to be offered? because the worshippers, having been once cleansed, would have had *no more* consciousness of sins" (Heb. 10.2).

"By which will we have been sanctified through the offering of the body of Jesus Christ *once* for all. And every priest indeed standeth day by day ministering and offering *oftentimes* the same sacrifices, the which can never take away sins: but he, when he had offered *one* sacrifice for sins for ever, sat down on the right hand of God" (Heb. 10.10–12).

Why do all the above passages indicate that the Lord Jesus has not offered himself many times but only once? It is because, beginning from Chapter 7, the book of Hebrews dwells on the comparison between the sacrifice which the

Lord Jesus has offered and the sacrifices offered in the Old Testament period. The Lord Jesus Christ has offered himself only once and has forever accomplished eternal redemption; whereas the sacrifices mentioned in the Old Testament were in the form of bulls and goats which were offered year by year. Individually speaking, anyone living in the dispensation of the Old Testament had to bring and offer a bullock or a goat or a pair of turtledoves or two young pigeons as a sin-offering each time he sinned. Corporately speaking, the whole congregation of Israel had to offer yearly, on the day of atonement, the sin-offering.

Why must they offer bulls and goats as sacrifices year after year? Because the blood of bulls and goats could never take away sins. People had to offer sacrifice for the sins of this year as well as the sins of last year. Only Jesus Christ through the *eternal* Spirit has offered himself to God, and by so doing has obtained *eternal* redemption so that He has perfected *forever* us who are sanctified (Heb. 9.14,12; 10.14).

Consequently, Hebrews 10 follows this up by saying that if anyone who has heard the truth and yet has sinned willfully has rejected the Holy Spirit as well as the blood of the Son of God. For such a person who has despised the Son of God there remains no more sacrifice for sins. For people in the Old Testament time, if they missed the opportunity for atonement one year they still might have it the following year. But today, if any man should reject Jesus Christ, there does not remain anymore sacrifice for sins, since even the sin-offering of the Old Testament dispensation has passed and is therefore no longer effective. Whoever has the knowledge of the truth but rejects it has no more sacrifice for sins available to him. For "in none other is there salvation" (Acts 4.12). God had done His uttermost when He sent the Lord Jesus Christ to this world to accomplish the work of redemption so that we might be saved. There is therefore nothing more He can add. Accordingly, the Bible tells us that if any man should sin willfully, that is, reject the gospel which he has heard and known, it is finished and done with for him. His end is nothing but a certain fearful expectation of judgment and a fierceness of fire which shall devour the adversaries.

Hebrews 6.1–8 says that the end of the class of people therein mentioned is "nigh to a curse"; but Hebrews 10.26–29 says that the result for its group of people is to be burned with the "fire which shall devour the adversaries"; how then can this latter group ever point to Christians? This passage can mean none but those who have knowingly rejected the gospel, therefore there is no other salvation. Otherwise, why should the word "more" be used in saying "there remaineth no more a sacrifice for sins"? Why should the word "once" be used repeatedly in the preceding verses? By joining these words within their context, we can easily discern the meaning of the words "there remaineth no more a sacrifice for sins".

Question 48

In the Bible, how many different kinds of forgiveness which come from God are mentioned? And what is their respective significance?

Answer:

Let us bear in mind this one factor: that the kind of consequence to sin will determine the kind of forgiveness involved. Now the consequences of sins are five in number:

(a) Eternal perdition.

(b) Separation from the people of God. (During the Old Testament days, if an Israelite sinned, he would be cut off from the congregation of the children of Israel. From the New Testament time onward there is also such a word as this: "Put away the wicked man from among yourselves"— 1 Cor. 5.13)

(c) Interruption in communion with God.

(d) If sin is not forsaken, there will be chastisement from God.

(e) If sin is not forsaken, it will adversely affect the person who has sinned, in the kingdom to come when the Lord shall reign and deal with such a problem.

(The fourth kind of consequence is chastisement in this age, whereas the fifth kind of consequence is a chastisement in the age to come. The Bible mentions in another context that "it shall not be forgiven him, neither in this world, nor in that which is to come". "World" here points to the "age". This gives us light on the truth that some sins are forgiven in this age while other sins are forgiven in the age to come.)

Since sins have these five different kinds of consequence, their forgiveness will also be of five different sorts. If there were only three kinds of forgiveness, what would happen to the other two consequences of sins remaining? So many people are confused in this regard, just as those are who think there is but one judgment. If we are not clear on these five different kinds of forgiveness we may sometimes become lost in a puzzle.

What are these five kinds of forgiveness? Let us first list them before attempting to explain each of them one by one.

(a) God's eternal forgiveness. (This concerns eternal salvation.)

(b) Forgiveness through God's people. (This concerns the fellowship of God's children. We may also call this forgiveness as borrowed forgiveness or the forgiveness of the church.)

(c) Forgiveness for the restoring of fellowship. (This concerns one's communion with God.)

(d) Forgiveness with discipline. (This concerns the way of God with His children.)

(e) Forgiveness in the kingdom. (This concerns the forgiveness during the millennial kingdom.)

Now let us explain them separately. (a) *God's eternal forgiveness.* Eternal forgiveness is related to man's eternal salvation. Although such forgiveness is for eternity, it nevertheless is given to a sinner today. On what basis is such forgiveness given? "Apart from shedding of blood there is no remission" (Heb. 9.22). "This is my blood of the covenant, which is poured out for many unto remission of sins" (Matt. 26.28). These verses tell us that eternal forgiveness is based on the blood of the Lord Jesus. No matter how big or gross a sin is, it can be forgiven through His blood. Such forgiveness is not without price, since God cannot freely forgive; for "apart from shedding of blood there is no remission", says His word. In forgiving our sins He has not overlooked them, for He *has* condemned sin. He can only forgive us because He has judged our sins in the flesh of Christ. The Lord Jesus has died, shed His precious blood, and paid the price. And so God can be most righteous in forgiving us, for how can He not forgive us since we have a Savior who has died for us?

The reason why our sins are forgiven is because the

Lamb of God has taken away our sins, because the blood of
Jesus God's Son has cleansed our sins. The basis for our
forgiveness is His blood; and through faith we receive this
forgiveness (Acts 10.43; 13.39). Do not vainly think that we
are forgiven because we have repented of our past sins and
have determined not to sin in the future. The word of God
tells us that our sins are forgiven because, and only because,
of the blood of the Lord Jesus. Whoever believes in His
blood shall see that his sins, having been laid on the Lord
Jesus, are all forgiven.

When do we receive the forgiveness of our sins—now or
in the future? "I write unto you, my little children, because
your sins are forgiven you for his name's sake" (1 John
2.12). Notice the words "are forgiven". It is not rendered
"waiting to be forgiven" but "are forgiven". Hallelujah! As
soon as a person believes in the Lord Jesus his sins are all
forgiven. God's word makes it clear: "My little children,
. . . your sins are forgiven you for his name's sake"; if God
says "are forgiven" they *are* forgiven, since He never lies.

(b) *Forgiveness through God's people.* "Whose soever sins ye
forgive, they are forgiven unto them; whose soever sins ye
retain, they are retained" (John 20.23). Is it not strange
concerning the forgiveness mentioned here? Does this mean
that the apostles have the authority on earth to forgive?
The answer to this question is very important, for if we do
not understand the meaning of this verse, we will not be
able to refute the presumed authority the pope claims to
have. The authority to forgive in relation to our salvation is
in the hand of God. Suppose, for instance, that you go to see
Peter and he refuses to forgive you. Does this mean to say
that you cannot be saved? Not at all, for salvation or the
forgiveness of sins is based on our accepting the precious
blood of the Lord Jesus.

Then to what does the forgiveness mentioned in John 20.23 refer? It refers to the declaration made by the church after she has been instructed by the Holy Spirit and has known the forgiveness of God given to an individual. We need to notice that the verse reads "whose soever sins *ye* forgive", with the pronoun stated in the plural number, not "you" in the singular. It is corporate, not personal; the church, not individual. "Whose soever sins ye forgive" means to say that when the church declares whose sins are forgiven, the person or persons involved were already saved people to begin with. Suppose a person should come to the church and say, "I have heard the gospel and have believed. Please receive me in baptism and in the breaking of bread that I may be like the other disciples." For the brethren to receive him, they need to know that his sins are forgiven by God. If the brethren know they are forgiven and that he is already a child of God, they will declare that he is indeed a forgiven and saved person, and he is therefore received into the fellowship of the church. If the brethren are not sure within themselves and cannot testify for him, they are not able to receive him. The forgiveness of the church is based on the forgiveness of God. The church merely declares what *God* has already done. And through the church God announces what the condition of the person is before Him.

We should pay attention to the verse preceding 23, since verse 23 follows and is a sequel to verse 22: "When he had said this, he breathed on them, and saith unto them, Receive ye the Holy Spirit" (v.22). The judgment the church makes concerning a person's forgiveness depends on the power of the Holy Spirit. She decides according to the teaching of the Holy Spirit, not according to personal feeling. Even if a person is truly saved and yet the church is not quite sure and so asks him to wait, this will in no wise affect his forgiveness before God. Take the instance of Paul who after he was saved and came to Jerusalem sought for fellowship with the disciples; but they were afraid of him and did not believe that he had really trusted in the Lord and had become a disciple of Christ. It was not until Barnabas bore him witness that he was able to go in and out with the disciples in Jerusalem (Acts 9.26–28). Hence the church itself does not *directly* forgive or retain a person's sins, she merely declares if one's sins are forgiven before God, thus deciding whether he is able to have fellowship among the disciples.

(c) *Forgiveness for restoring fellowship.* "My little children, these things write I unto you that ye may not sin. And if any man sin, we have an Advocate with the Father, Jesus Christ the righteous: and he is the propitiation for our sins; and not for ours only, but also for the whole world" (1 John 2.1,2). "If we confess our sins, he is faithful and righteous to forgive us our sins, and to cleanse us from all unrighteousness" (1 John 1.9). Let us first be clear on the emphasis of John's Gospel and of his earliest epistle. The Gospel of John discloses the gospel among men, while the First Epistle of John reveals the gospel in God's heart. John's Gospel runs along two lines of thought—grace and truth: when it speaks on grace it speaks also on truth. The First Epistle of John also runs along two lines of thought—God is love and God is light: it speaks of love on the one hand and of light on the other. What is the relationship of grace and truth with love and light? That which is in the heart of God is love; that which is expressed among men is grace. What is in God's heart is light; what is manifested among men is truth.

The Gospel of John brings God to the people, but the First Epistle of John brings the people to God. The Gospel speaks of life, salvation, eternal life, and other similar matters and the First Epistle speaks of fellowship, drawing nigh to God, and coming into His presence. The Gospel deals with the question of salvation, whereas the First Epistle deals with the question of communion with God. The Epistle opens up with the matter of fellowship, both Chapters 1 and 2 dwelling on the forgiveness in fellowship.

Our relationship to God is two-fold. The first one is the kindred relationship we have with God: we are saved and thus become His children. This relationship can *never* be broken. Question No. 1—Will a son cease to be a son if he is bad? No, impossible. Question No. 2—Will a son cease to be a son of his father because he is unwilling to be such a son? No, he cannot. Question No. 3—Will a son cease to be a son to his father if the latter denies him? No, he will not. Question No. 4—Suppose you are son to a certain man, can other people or the devil oppose your being his son? No, they cannot. Let us say reverently that not even God himself can deny this relationship. After a person is born again and becomes a child of God, this relationship can never be overturned, since such a relationship is eternally secured.

Nevertheless, there *is* a kind of relationship which *may* be interrupted from time to time. That relationship is the one of fellowship. For example, you are your father's son. But one day you do something wrong. So you are afraid to see him lest you be scolded. And the greater your fault, the more you are afraid to see him. Even though your relationship as kindred remains unbroken, your communication with him is interrupted. So too is our relationship with God. There is still the possibility of sinning after we are saved. As we sin, our fellowship with God is immediately cut. Such fellowship is not restored until our sins are forgiven. If we sin, we must confess our sins according to 1 John 1.9, acknowledging that we have done wrong in a certain matter and asking God to forgive us. By such confession our fellowship with Him will be restored.

By what means are sins cleansed? By the blood. Nonetheless, many Christians try to cleanse their sins by means of time and not by the blood. How so? Well, a person who sins today might continually moan for several days because he thinks that God cannot so quickly forgive. After five or ten days of this his heart begins to feel peaceful, so he concludes that there is no more sin. Is not this an attempt to cleanse one's sins away with five or ten days of time rather than with the blood? Let us be clear that our sins are forgiven because of the blood and not because of forgetting. Not because we have forgotten our sins are our sins forgiven; only because the blood of Jesus God's Son has cleansed us from all our sins. God can only forgive sins that are under the blood.

There was once a story that ran like this: Someone asked a child what he would do if he sinned. He replied that he must do two things: first, he must grieve for a few days; then, he would receive forgiveness. The theology of this child seems to be that of many people. It appears to them as though there must be enough grief and time to have elapsed before there can be forgiveness. Brothers and sisters, no matter how many days you spend in grieving, they will not help you obtain even one one-hundredth of your forgiveness. It is right and proper for us to feel sorrow for our sins, yet our forgiveness does not come by our grieving but only by the blood of the Lord Jesus, and thus shall our fellowship with Him be restored.

(d) *Forgiveness with discipline.* This pertains to God's way of dealing with His children. What is His dealing? It is His way, that is to say, it is the manner by which He will deal with people. Let us first read several passages in the Bible.

"With the merciful thou wilt show thyself merciful; with the perfect man thou wilt show thyself perfect; with the pure thou will show thyself pure; and with the perverse thou will show thyself froward" (2 Sam. 22.26,27). This is a description of God's way of dealing. He will deal with you in accordance with what you are. "Be not deceived; God is not mocked: for whatsoever a man soweth, that shall he also reap. For he that soweth unto his own flesh shall of the flesh reap corruption; but he that soweth unto the Spirit shall of the Spirit reap eternal life" (Gal. 6.7,8). These verses too show us the principle by which God deals with people. He who sows to the flesh shall of the flesh reap corruption; but he who sows to the Spirit shall of the Spirit reap eternal life. In our sinning, there is not only a crime committed before God, there is likewise a suffering which is an accompaniment or an aftermath of sin. The crime may be forgiven but the suffering cannot be avoided. A child disobeys his mother by stealing candies to eat. If he repents, the crime of stealing candies may be forgiven but his teeth will soon be decayed. Frequently God's children have their sins forgiven, yet they must reap the effect of these sins. Eternal forgiveness is given as soon as one believes; forgiveness for the restoration of fellowship is granted immediately after one confesses, but God's dealing in connection with such forgiveness is something quite painful.

Take Samson as an example. He was a leader and judge over God's people. Later he fell into sin and was ill-treated by the Philistines. Though he made a last request to Jehovah, saying "O Lord Jehovah, remember me, I pray thee, and strengthen me, I pray thee, only this once, O God, that I may be at once avenged of the Philistines for my two eyes" (Judges 16.28), and though he slew more at his death than during his entire lifetime, yet his eyes were never restored. His hair might grow again, his fellowship with

God might be recovered, but his office as a judge is not restored.

In 2 Samuel 11 we find recorded that David committed two of the grossest kinds of sin—adultery and murder. God sent the prophet Nathan to reprove him, and God most severely judged his sins:

> Now therefore the sword shall never depart from thy house, because thou hast despise me, and hast taken the wife of Uriah the Hittite to be thy wife. . . . I will raise up evil against thee out of thine own house, and I will take thy wives before thine eyes, and give them unto thy neighbor, and he shall lie with thy wives in the sight of this sun. For thou didst it secretly: but I will do this thing before all Israel, and before the sun. (2 Sam. 12.10–12)

This was what David received under God's discipline. For although David confessed his sin and was told by Nathan that "Jehovah also hath put away thy sin", he had to undergo suffering under discipline. By confessing to God, his sin was forgiven and his fellowship with Him was restored, yet discipline followed upon the heels of forgiveness. He murdered but one Uriah, but four of his sons died (the first child born to Bathsheba, and also Ammon, Absalom, and Adonijah). This is the righteous act of God. In knowing this, we dare not sin. God had to vindicate himself to the effect that He was displeased with what David did. If God did not discipline David for his sin the whole world would say that God was pleased with David's conduct. God could forgive David, but He must express His detestation of David's sin.

"Is any among you sick? let him call for the elders of the church; and let them pray over him, anointing him with oil in the name of the Lord: and the prayer of faith shall save him that is sick, and the Lord shall raise him up; and if he have committed sins, it shall be forgiven him" (James 5.14,15). The forgiveness cited here is a forgiveness which is under discipline. Were this a reference to eternal forgiveness, how could it be obtained through the prayer of faith of other people? But then too, this cannot be the forgiveness for restoring fellowship because a person's own confession alone will instantly bring it about. A forgiveness under discipline is to be implemented by asking the elders of the church to come, and, if the Lord gives them the prayer of faith, the sick shall be made well.

"He was wounded for our transgressions, he was bruised for our iniquities; the chastisement of our peace was upon him; and with his stripes we are healed" (Is. 53.5). This verse touches on four different areas: (1) pertaining to works, (2) pertaining to the condition before God, (3) pertaining to the body, and (4) pertaining to God's discipline—for the pertinent clause may also be translated "he was chastised for the sake of our peace". The Lord has already been chastised for us; there is therefore this element of chastisement in the work of the cross. Consequently, we may ask God to dispense with our chastisement since the Lord has already been chastised.

> Be subject therefore unto God; but resist the devil, and he will flee from you. (James 4.7) Humble yourselves therefore under the mighty hand of God, that he may exalt you in due time, casting all your anxiety upon him, because he careth for you. Be sober, be watchful: your adversary the devil, as a roaring lion, walketh about, seeking whom he may devour: whom withstand stedfast in your faith, knowing that the same sufferings are accomplished in your brethren who are in the world. And the God of all grace, who called you unto his eternal glory in Christ, after that ye have suffered a little while, shall himself perfect, establish, strengthen you. (1 Peter 5.6–10)

Whenever we are disciplined, let us humble ourselves under the mighty hand of God. Let us say to Him: "I will not resist what You give me; I deserve the treatment You give me." Yet we must indeed resist the devil, because if we are not careful he will give us additional sufferings which are totally unwarranted. When God chastises, the devil tries to attack; we must therefore resist the devil. Only after we have humbled ourselves under the discipline of God are we able to resist the devil. On the one hand we must obey God; on the other hand we must exercise our will daily to resist the devil, declaring that we refuse to be sick or weak.

(e) *Forgiveness in the kingdom.* Concerning the forgiveness in the kingdom we may read Matthew 18.21–35:

> Then came Peter and said to him, Lord, how oft shall my brother sin against me, and I forgive him? until seven times? Jesus saith unto him, I say not unto thee, Until seven times; but, Until seventy times seven. Therefore is the kingdom of heaven likened unto a certain king, who would make a reckoning with his servants. And when he had begun to reckon, one was brought unto him, that owed him ten thousand talents. But forasmuch as he had not wherewith to pay, his lord commanded him to be sold, and his wife, and children, and all that he had, and payment to be made. The servant therefore fell down and worshipped him, saying, Lord, have patience with me, and I will pay thee all. And the Lord of that servant, being moved with compassion, released him, and forgave him the debt. But that servant went out, and found one of his fellow-servants, who owed him a hundred shillings: and he laid hold on him, and took him by the throat, saying, Pay what thou owest. So his fellow-servant fell down and besought him, saying, Have patience with me, and I will pay thee. And he would not: but went and cast him into prison, till he should pay that which was due. So when his fellow-servants saw what was done, they were exceeding sorry, and came and told unto

their lord all that was done. Then his lord called him unto
him, and saith to him, Thou wicked servant, I forgave thee
all that debt, because thou besoughtest me: shouldest not
thou also have had mercy on thy fellow-servant, even as I
had mercy on thee? And his lord was wroth, and delivered
him to the tormentors, till he should pay all that was due. So
shall also my heavenly Father do unto you, if ye forgive not
every one his brother from your hearts.

In reading the Bible we will be confronted by a great
difficulty if we are unable to distinguish the various kinds of
forgiveness. Unless we can distinguish what kind of forgiveness we have in this particular case we will most likely
speculate that our heavenly Father might rescind eternal
forgiveness and allow us to become unsaved. We ought to
know that the forgiveness spoken of here does not fall into
any of the four preceding categories but pertains to the
forgiveness in the kingdom. Such a category of forgiveness
will be received in a way similar to the way found in the
above parable which begins: "The kingdom of heaven [is]
likened unto a certain king, who would make a reckoning
with his servants" (v.23). Concerning the church God
speaks of grace; concerning the kingdom, He speaks of
responsibility. As regards the church, we are told what the
Lord has done and how He treats us; as regards the
kingdom, we are shown how we are trained before God,
how we live today, and what will be the judgment in the
future. Here in Matthew 18 we are shown our responsibility, for this passage is concerned with the kingdom of
heaven—with reigning for a thousand years—and not with
the question of eternal salvation.

There are a number of parables on the kingdom in the
four gospels, and Matthew 18.21–35 is one of them. Here
the kingdom of heaven is likened to a certain king who
reckons with his servants. One servant owed his lord ten

thousand talents and was not able to repay the debt. He begged his lord for patience that he might pay him back later. His lord was moved with compassion and forgave him the debt. But when the servant came out and met his fellow-servant who owed him a mere hundred shillings, he would not forgive him but put him into prison till he paid back all he owed. Afterward, other fellow-servants told this matter to the lord, and the lord said to him: "Shouldst not thou also have had mercy on thy fellow-servant, even as I had mercy on thee?" (v.33) Having finished relating this parable, the Lord Jesus began to explain it. Said the Lord, "So shall also my heavenly Father do unto you, if ye forgive not every one his brother from your hearts" (v.35). This is about the forgiveness in the kingdom. Such forgiveness is not the portion of all Christians, for it is given only to those Christians who forgive others.

Let us pause here and recapitulate what we have learned about forgiveness. The first kind of forgiveness is received through believing in the Lord Jesus. The second kind is obtained through the declaration of the church. The third is given upon confessing our sins to God. The fourth is granted after God reckons that the time of chastisement is fulfilled and He removes the rod. But the fifth kind of forgiveness, the one now under consideration, is bestowed after we have forgiven other people from our hearts.

We know that the daily life and work of a Christian on earth will be judged in the future. After the rapture all Christians will stand judgment before the judgment seat of Christ. This is not to be a judging of the salvation of a Christian but the judging of his fitness for the kingdom and his position in the kingdom. Thus there are two perils in our standing before the judgment seat: first, we may be barred completely from the kingdom; or, second, we may receive a *low* position in the kingdom if we *are* allowed to enter.

How will God judge? The kingdom is God's reward, and reward must be determined by our works. Though we cannot be saved through good works, we still need good works to be rewarded. Our salvation is due to faith, our reward is due to good works.

There was once a saint who said: "I ask God to cleanse with the blood of the Lord my penitent tears for sins! I ask God to wash with the blood of the Lord my sorrowful repentance!" One day at the judgment seat, the Lord's eyes as a flame of fire will search our lives and works through and through from the very day we were saved and all the time thereafter. At that moment of judgment, perhaps there will be very few things which shall be reckoned by the Lord as being faultless. For what might be viewed by many of us as constituting most excellent works will instead be judged by the Lord as being unclean and worldly-wise and impure. Many so-called "good" works may be condemned as being very bad.

Since judgment is to begin at the house of God (1 Peter 4.17), how serious must be this judgment! And if so, who can pass this judgment? How must we expect God to be merciful to us at the judgment seat, for even there we need grace! This is exactly what Matthew 18 is talking about. It is true that God will judge us with absolute justice; nevertheless, there *is* forgiveness with Him, and His forgiveness is based on our forgiving others today. No matter how people may treat you, if you forgive five or ten persons who sin against you and you always forgive, then in that day God will treat you justly. Because you have forgiven others, it is most just for God to forgive you at the judgment seat.

"Judgment is without mercy to him that hath showed no mercy: mercy glorieth against judgment" (James 2.13). If you show mercy to others God will also show mercy to you. If you show no mercy neither will God show you mercy. By treating people generously, without being cruel or captious, you will be forgiven by God too on that day.

We need to be careful daily about two things: one is to examine ourselves lest we fall into the judgment of God; and the other is, that however much people may owe us, let us be merciful and forgiving so that we may receive God's forgiveness on that day.

"Judge not, that ye be not judged. For with what judgment ye judge, ye shall be judged" (Matt. 7.1,2). According to the manner in which you judge people so will God judge you. The way you judge your brothers will become the way that He will judge you. Suppose you notice something wrong in a person. Instead of lovingly persuading him, you render to him only hard criticism and harsh judgment. On that day God will judge you in the same manner. Hence the way God will judge you on the day of judgment depends on how you today treat other people. This likewise is the meaning of the first few verses in Romans 2:

> Thou art without excuse, O man, whosoever thou art that judgest: for wherein thou judgest another, thou condemnest thyself; for thou that judgest dost practise the same things. And we know that the judgment of God is according to truth against them that practise such things. And reckonest thou this, O man, who judgest them that practise such things, and doest the same, that thou shalt escape the judgment of God? (vv.1–3)

"Give and it shall be given unto you; good measure, pressed down, shaken together, running over, shall they give into your bosom. For with what measure ye mete it shall be measured to you again" (Luke 6.38). These words in Luke are very clear. If we give, God will repay abundantly in shaking together and running over. The measure is not only good measure and pressed down but also shaken together and running over. In the measure of grace you give to others God shall give you the same measure of grace. It is absolutely impossible for you to expect God to deal graciously with you in the future if you treat others sharply today. In view of this, let all Christians learn not to judge. Do not consider yourself as being just and right enough to judge. If we do not forgive others we shall receive severe punishment in the thousand years of the kingdom. There is no doubt that eternal life for us is certain and secure, because eternal salvation is what we get; if, though, we do not forgive our debtors in this life then in the future kingdom God will not forgive us either.

How is a nation destroyed? How is a house fallen? Is it not due to internal strife? For this reason God will not allow any striving among His own, nor will He permit any hatred to exist. How can He tolerate any enmity between two people who each are to rule five cities? He cannot allow the discordant ones to rule over cities. He can only deliver them to the tormentors until they have paid all that is due. How will the payment be made? In no other way than that they will forgive from their hearts. In that case, why should we postpone forgiving until that day, since we shall have to forgive eventually anyway?

"If ye forgive men their trespasses, your heavenly Father will also forgive you. But if ye forgive not men their trespasses, neither will your Father forgive your trespasses" (Matt. 6.14,15). Matthew Chapters 5, 6 and 7 speak of the kingdom of heaven. Whoever does not forgive other men shall not be forgiven by God. Such forgiveness will affect his place in the kingdom. Whether he forgives or not today will bear on whether he is forgiven or not in the kingdom.

Our God is now testing us to see if we are fit to be kings in His kingdom, to see if we are worthy to minister in His kingdom. Do not think that serving in the church is great; service in the kingdom is even greater. In the future kingdom God will commit higher and more glorious things to us to administer. Whoever is unable to manage small things now is unfit to manage great things then. If we do not know how to deal with matters of this life, how can we be trusted to judge the angels in the future (see 1 Cor. 6.1–8)? For the sake of that day let us learn to forgive others in our own day.

Question 49

How many kinds of salvation are mentioned in the Bible? What are their explanations?

Answer:

The Bible mentions at least six different kinds of salvation. (a) *Eternally saved before God.* This first kind of salvation is eternal salvation before God. This we receive the moment we believe in the Lord Jesus. It is our being delivered from the judgment of sins, the curse of the law, the threat of death, the punishment of hell, and the power of Satan. It also speaks of our being justified, sanctified, and reconciled to God as well as of our sins being forgiven and our iniquities cleansed. It means too that we are now born again, possessing the eternal life of the Lord, with our spirit quickened and the Holy Spirit indwelling us. We are so wonderfully saved purely by the grace of God, it having absolutely nothing to do with our works. "By grace have ye been saved through faith; and that not of yourselves, it is the gift of God; not of works, that no man should glory" (Eph. 2.8,9). "Who saved us, and called us with a holy calling, not according to our works, but according to his own purpose and grace" (2 Tim. 1.9a). "Not by works done in righteousness, which we did ourselves, but according to his mercy he saved us" (Titus 3.5a). "We believe that we shall be saved through the grace of the Lord Jesus" (Acts 15.11a).

This eternal salvation is accomplished for us by the Lord Jesus. He is our Savior who came to die for us, who bore our sins in His body upon the tree (1 Peter 2.24) in order to redeem us from the curse of the law (Gal. 3.13), to deliver us from the wrath to come (1 Thess. 1.10), to bring to nought the devil who has the power of death (Heb. 2.14), to liberate us from the power of darkness (Col. 1.13), and to cause us to escape judgment and pass out of death into life (John 5.24). By the resurrection of the Lord Jesus from the dead we are born again and are given eternal life that we might be children of God (1 Peter 1.3; John 1.12). By His ascension we are brought to God the Father with whom we now have fellowship in the holiest place (Heb. 9.12; 10.19–22), far above all the powers of darkness (Eph. 1.21). All these are done wholly by the Lord; we only receive, that is, we believe in Him: "As many as received him, to them gave he the right to become children of God, even to them that believe on his name" (John 1.12). The gospel "is the power of God unto salvation to every one that believeth" (Rom. 1.16). "Believe on the Lord Jesus, and thou shalt be saved, thou and thy house" (Acts 16.31).

Such kind of salvation is eternal. Once saved, forever saved. "Having been made perfect, he became unto all them that obey him the author of eternal salvation" (Heb. 5.9). The salvation which the Lord has accomplished for us is eternal, therefore our salvation is also eternal.

As regards the security of our salvation—that is to say, we will never perish once we are saved—we can find at least twelve different areas of evidence in the Scriptures.

(1) *According to God's will*—God foreordained us to be His children and to have sonship given to us, yet not according to our conditions but according to the good pleasure of His will (Eph. 1.5). He saves us and calls us with a holy calling, yet not according to our works but according to His own purpose (2 Tim. 1.9). For our conditions may change, but God's will never changes (Heb. 6.17). In eternity He has formed a will which wills to save us that none of us should be lost (John 6.39). How then can we be saved and later be unsaved? Our salvation is forever secured in the unchangeable will of God.

(2) *According to God's election*—God's choosing us is neither accidental nor temporary. He has chosen us in Christ before the foundation of the world (Eph. 1.4). His election is not according to our works but according to His will (Rom. 9.11). For we have not chosen the Lord; the Lord has chosen us (John 15.16). Just as the Lord never changes, so His election knows no repentance (Rom. 11.29). Hence our salvation is eternally secured and will never be moved.

(3) *According to God's love*—Our salvation is based on God's love for us and not our love for God (1 John 4.10). Our love changes easily, but God's love is deeper than a mother's (Is. 49.15). It is eternal (Jer. 31.1), to the end (John 13.1), and changeless. This everlasting love of God has made His salvation eternally secured to us.

(4) *According to God's grace*—We are saved, not by ourselves nor by our own works but by the grace of God (Eph. 2.8,9). We ourselves with our works often change, but the grace of God is firm and sure. For this reason our salvation is eternally secured. Furthermore, this saving

grace is given to us in Christ Jesus even before the foundation of the world (2 Tim. 1.9), and we have our redemption according to the riches of God's grace (Eph. 1.7). His grace is always sufficient and more than sufficient. His grace is able to bear all our burdens, supply all our needs, and save us to the uttermost.

(5) *According to God's righteousness*—God saves us not only by His love and grace but also according to His righteousness. He cannot help but save us, because the Lord Jesus on our behalf has already suffered on the cross the righteous judgment of God and has satisfied God's righteous demands. Therefore, if God will not save us He will fall into unrighteousness. In saving us He reveals that He is righteous (Rom. 1.16,17), for righteousness is the foundation of His throne (Ps. 89.14). His righteousness is immovable. Since our justification is founded on the righteousness of God, it is eternal and immovable.

(6) *According to God's covenant*—God has made a covenant with us to save us (Matt. 26.28; Heb. 8.8–12), and a covenant can suffer no alteration (Ps. 89.34). And hence our salvation cannot be changed.

(7) *According to God's power*—"My Father who hath given them unto me, is greater than all; and no one is able to snatch them out of the Father's hand" (John 10.29). God is supreme and His power is the greatest; none can snatch us out of His mighty hand. So that according to His power our salvation is also secured.

(8) *According to God's life*—God's life is eternal. God has given this eternal life to us that we may become His children and have an everlasting life relationship with Him (John 3.16; 1 John 3.1). *Life* relationship can never be dissolved. His eternal life in us will not allow us to perish (John 10.28).

(9) *According to God himself*—There is no variation nor

shadow of turning with God (James 1.17; Mal. 3.6). How can our salvation ever waver then, since it comes from such a God?

(10) *According to the redemption of Christ*—The Lord has become to us the author of eternal salvation (Heb. 5.9). We are sanctified through the offering of the body of Jesus Christ once for all (Heb. 10.14). Since what the Lord has done is eternal, our salvation must also be eternal. Because of this, "who is he that condemneth? It is Christ Jesus that died, yea rather, that was raised from the dead, who is at the right hand of God, who also maketh intercession for us" (Rom. 8.34). None can abrogate the redemption which the Lord through His death and resurrection has accomplished for us. None can condemn us for our sins. Hence our salvation is eternally secured.

(11) *According to the power of Christ*—"No one shall snatch them out of my hand" (John 10.28). The Lord and God are one. He is equal with God, therefore His hand is as strong as God's hand. No one can snatch us out of His hand. His almighty hand makes our salvation eternally secured.

(12) *According to the promise of Christ*—"Him that cometh to me I will in no wise cast out" (John 6.37). The Lord has promised that He will never cast out any of us who come to Him. Such a promise of His likewise guarantees our eternal salvation.

(b) *Saved before men.* "He that believeth and is baptized shall be saved" (Mark 16.16). The word "saved" here does not refer to eternal salvation, since the latter part of the same verse reads: "but he that disbelieveth shall be condemned". Why does the latter part not say "he that disbelieveth and is not baptized shall be condemned" even as the earlier part says that "he that believeth and is baptized shall be saved"? By omitting baptism while speaking about condemnation the writer has indicated to us that the word "saved" in the first part does not have reference to the same thing as do the words "not condemned" in the second part. Not condemned is wholly a matter of faith, whereas, in this instance, to be saved requires both faith *and* baptism. Consequently, the salvation in Mark 16.16 cannot refer to the eternal salvation of not being condemned. Then to what does it refer? It refers to our salvation before men. If a person merely believes without being baptized—and though he may have eternal life in him—the world will not know that he is a saved man. He must rise up and be baptized, thus declaring to the world that his sins are forgiven and he is now separated from it. Hence the salvation in baptism points to the salvation before men.

(c) *Saved daily.* "Work out your own salvation with fear and trembling" (Phil. 2.12). We are saved not by what we ourselves have accomplished but by the grace of God freely given to us. But it is said here that we must work out our own salvation. We are already saved; therefore, in our lives we must live out the salvation we have already received. As soon as we believe in the Lord we receive God's life, and God dwells in us by the Holy Spirit. For it is God who works in us both to will and to do of His good pleasure (Phil. 2.13). In this way we will live out the life of God and daily live in obedience to His working in us. Such kind of life will not be arrived at instantaneously but will require living daily with fear and trembling.

"He is able to save to the uttermost them that draw near unto God through him, seeing he ever liveth to make intercession for them" (Heb. 7.25). We are told how the Lord will save us daily in our lives. He is today interceding for us before God that we might be preserved and delivered until the day of His coming.

There is yet one more thing we need to take note of concerning this daily salvation. The Lord wants us to pray daily, asking God to deliver us from the evil one (Matt. 6.13). As Satan tries daily and frequently to tempt, entice, attack, and harm us, we must daily and frequently look to the Lord for deliverance.

(d) *Saved out of afflictions.* This kind of salvation pertains to the deliverance which God gives us in afflictions. "Who delivered us out of so great a death, and will deliver: on whom we have set out hope that he will also still deliver us" (2 Cor. 1.10). The salvation here spoken of does not point to the eternal salvation before God; it follows the trend of thought in verses 8 and 9. Paul is talking about how he and his fellow-workers were afflicted in Asia, weighed down exceedingly beyond their power, insomuch that they despaired even of life itself. They had the sentence of death within themselves, yet God delivered them out of so great an affliction and death. He had delivered them in the past, He is now delivering them, and He will yet deliver them in the future. God will deliver them out of all afflictions.

"The angel of Jehovah encampeth round about them that fear him, and delivereth them" (Ps. 34.7). God will order His angels to encamp around those who fear Him and will deliver them out of their afflictions.

"I know that this shall turn out to my salvation, through your supplication and the supply of the Spirit of Jesus" (Phil. 1.19). "I was delivered out of the mouth of the lion. The Lord will deliver me from every evil work" (2 Tim. 4.17b,18a). All these passages refer to our being saved out of afflictions and evils.

(e) *Saved in body.* At the second coming of the Lord our body shall be redeemed, transformed, and conformed to His glorious body (Phil. 3.21). This too is called salvation in the Bible, and here it is that of the body. We "ourselves also, who have the first-fruits of the Spirit, even we ourselves groan within ourselves, waiting for our adoption, to wit, the redemption of our body" (Rom. 8.23). This is immediately followed by "For in hope were we saved" (v.24). The word "saved" in verse 24 refers to "the redemption of our body" in verse 23. Since the redemption of the body is to be brought to pass at the second coming of the Lord, we must therefore hope for it. At the time we first believed in the Lord we received eternal salvation and our spirit was quickened; even so, our body is still groaning and travailing in pain in the old creation because it is still subject to the bondage of corruption and the pains of sickness and age. When the Lord returns He will redeem this body of ours—which as a part of the old creation is subject to bondage—and transform it and lead it into the glorious liberty of the new creation.

"Now is salvation nearer to us than when we first believed" (Rom. 13.11). This too points to the salvation of the body. Our spirit is saved when we first believe; but our body is to be saved in the future. Once we have believed, the time of the salvation of our body draws nearer and nearer to us.

(f) *Saved in soul.* We as human beings are made of three parts: spirit, soul, and body (1 Thess. 5.23). Our salvation therefore reaches into each of these three areas. The salvation of our spirit is received through the regeneration of the Holy Spirit at the time we believe in the Lord. God forgives all our sins and the Holy Spirit comes into us and quickens our dead spirit. The salvation of our body will

happen at the coming of the Lord when He "shall fashion
anew the body of our humiliation, that it may be conformed
to the body of his glory, according to the working whereby
he is able even to subject all things to himself" (Phil. 3.21).
But besides these two parts of our being our soul also needs
to be saved; and its salvation is related especially to our
entering the millennial kingdom and reigning with the
Lord, who will reward us and cause our soul to enjoy with
Him the joy of the kingdom.

"Whosoever would save his life [soul] shall lose it: and
whosoever shall lose his life [soul] for my sake shall find it"
(Matt. 16.25). "Save" here does not point to eternal
salvation, since the salvation spoken of here is not something freely given according to faith. The salvation before
us here requires a cost—the soul shall be saved by losing and
sacrificing itself. A saved person who is willing to deny
himself, to take up the cross and follow the Lord, and to be
willing to sacrifice his own soul shall enter the millennial
kingdom and rejoice with the Lord (Matt. 25.21,23). The
soul is the site of man's feeling, whether joy or pain. If a
person endures pain and sacrifices temporary pleasure for
the Lord's sake, he shall enjoy the joy of the Lord at His
coming. Man's soul is his own self. He who is willing to lose
his own self today for the sake of the Lord shall be given
what is really his own in the future (Luke 16.11,12).

"Whosoever would save his life [soul] shall lose it; and
whosoever shall lose his life [soul] for my sake and the
gospel's shall save it" (Mark 8.35). The Lord's cause and
that of the gospel's are often connected in God's word and
are therefore inseparable. If today we sacrifice the soul
and its pleasure for either the Lord's sake or the gospel's
sake, our soul will gain special joy in the future kingdom,
because we shall reign with the Lord and enjoy His joy in
glory.

"Whosoever shall seek to gain his life [soul] shall lose it; but whosoever shall lose his life [soul] shall preserve it" (Luke 17.33). Believers who seek to gain their souls with its pleasures in this life shall lose all pleasures during the kingdom. But all who lose their souls and its pleasures in this world for the sake of the Lord shall have their souls saved and shall enjoy greatly in the kingdom.

"He that endureth to the end, the same shall be saved" (Matt. 10.22). "In your patience ye shall win your souls" (Luke 21.19). Believers who will endure persecution to the end shall be rewarded by the Lord in the day to come. Their souls shall not suffer but shall have joy.

"We are not of them that shrink back unto perdition; but of them that have faith unto the saving of the soul" (Heb. 10.39). The "faith" here mentioned is the faith we exercise after we have believed in the Lord Jesus. It is not the faith for entry, but the faith for walking; not the faith for life, but the faith for living. If after we are saved we should walk in the way of the Lord by faith and live a victorious life, our souls shall be saved in the future and we shall have a part in the glory and joy of the kingdom.

"Receiving the end of your faith, even the salvation of your souls" (1 Peter 1.9). The "faith" here is again the faith we exercise after we are saved; it is the faith by which to live. Such faith will preserve us through difficulties and trials, and will prepare our souls to receive the salvation which shall appear at the second coming of the Lord—even the deliverance from all sorrows and the enjoyment of the glorious joy of the kingdom.

"Putting away all filthiness and overflowing of wickedness, receive with meekness the implanted word, which is able to save your souls" (James 1.21). The salvation of the soul is different from the salvation of the spirit. In the latter case nothing is required of us except to believe and to receive it. In the former case, however, we are asked to put off all filthiness and overflowing of wickedness and to receive with meekness the implanted word.

"The Lord . . . will save me unto his heavenly kingdom" (2 Tim. 4.18). "If ye do these things, ye shall never stumble: for thus shall be richly supplied unto you the entrance into the eternal kingdom of our Lord and Saviour Jesus Christ" (2 Peter 1.10,11). The salvation of the soul means a being delivered into the kingdom of heaven which is the eternal kingdom of our Lord and Savior Jesus Christ.

Question 50

What is the meaning of sanctification? How are we sanctified?

Answer:

Concerning sanctification, let us notice the following three points. (a) *The meaning of sanctification.* From the Old Testament to the New, from Genesis to Revelation, wherever the word "sanctify" (or related words) is mentioned, it always denotes "set apart to", that is, to set apart in order to belong to another.

"Jehovah spake unto Moses, saying, Sanctify unto me all the first-born, whatsoever openeth the womb among the children of Israel, both of man and of beast: it is mine" (Ex. 13.1,2). All the firstborn among the children of Israel are God's since they are set apart to Him. They are holy, they belong to Him. So the meaning of sanctification is to be set apart to God. Things can also be sanctified to Him (Lev.

27.14; 2 Sam. 8.11). The Lord Jesus is sanctified by the Father (John 10.36). He is "the holy thing" (Luke 1.35). He is different from all other men in that He is "the only begotten Son, who is in the bosom of the Father" (John 1.18) and is holy. We who believe in the Lord are called saints (Acts 9.13), which word means that we are sanctified to be holy to God.

While on earth the Lord Jesus asked the Pharisees, "Which is greater, the gift, or the altar that sanctifieth the gift?" (Matt. 23.19) It is not the gift which sanctifies the altar, rather is it that the altar sanctifies the gift. By placing it on the altar a person is declaring that the gift now belongs to God. Before it is offered on the altar it belongs to one's own self; but after it is offered, it belongs to God. This does not suggest that the thing itself has changed; but it does announce that it has now become God's entirely. Hence, it is holy. In the Old Testament the tabernacle with all its many objects are anointed so as to be sanctified. This does not mean that these objects have intrinsically been changed; but it does denote that these things now wholly belong to God for His use, and therefore they are holy. The New Testament also declares that an unbelieving husband is sanctified through the believing wife, that an unbelieving wife is sanctified through the believing husband, and that the unbelieving children are made holy through the believing parents (1 Cor. 7.14). This too shows that though nothing in these persons themselves has changed, yet they are now sanctified through their believing husband, wife, or parents.

Since God has purchased us with the blood of the Lord Jesus we no longer can belong to other people. We are set apart to God, and we belong to Him alone.

(b) *The sanctified position before God.* Every Christian, at the time he receives the Lord, not only has had his sins forgiven and has become justified but also has been sanctified before God. God is holy; without holiness no man can see Him, commune with Him, or pray before Him. As righteousness is God's way of doing things, so holiness is His nature. Sins are forgiven according to righteousness. Without forgiveness of sins no one can be saved. And without holiness none may see God (Heb. 12.14). Holiness is not a matter relating to sins, it relates to our being set apart to God. Because every Christian is sanctified in Christ, he therefore may come to God.

Romans deals with justification, but Hebrews deals with sanctification. Romans speaks of righteousness, while Hebrews speaks of holiness. Romans centers on the throne, whereas Hebrews centers on the holiest of all. Romans tells how man is guilty before God; Hebrews tells how man is unclean before Him. Though forgiveness and justification take away a Christian's guiltiness and enable him to stand before God, still, without holiness he is not able to enjoy His presence and to commune with Him in the holiest.

Romans informs us that we are sinners but that God has forgiven our sins and justified us through the death of His Son. Hebrews instructs us that our body is unclean but that the blood of the Son of God has washed us so that by His blood we may enter the holiest place and commune with God. We have holiness to enter the holiest by the blood of the Lord Jesus.

How inclusive is sanctification? God's gospel always draws forth hallelujahs. God is holy. And holiness is His highest glory. In Christ we are as holy as He is. This is the highest. Anything less than this will bar us from coming to God. But because in Christ we are as holy as Christ is, therefore we can come before God who looks on us as He would look on Christ. Thank God, how perfect and how everlasting is the redemption of Jesus Christ. Were it not perfect, the righteousness of God would not come upon us. Were it not everlasting, we would not be sanctified forever unto God. The redemption of the Lord Jesus being perfect and everlasting, we may receive eternal forgiveness and be sanctified forever unto God.

"Unto the church of God which is at Corinth, even them that are sanctified in Christ Jesus, called to be saints, with all that call upon the name of our Lord Jesus Christ in every place, their Lord and ours" (1 Cor. 1.2). Paul wrote to the Corinthians, who were sanctified in Christ Jesus and called to be saints. Now the phrase translated "called to be saints" is in the original rendered "called saints". We are not called to be saints; we are saints by calling, meaning we are already sanctified to God. As soon as we are called we are saved, sanctified in Christ, and called saints.

May we not legitimately ask, then, what kind of believers the Corinthians were? Some consumed their own food and drink before they partook of the table of the Lord—so that while these were overly filled or even drunk, others in the church went hungry. Yet at the very beginning of his first letter to them Paul conceded that they were sanctified in Christ Jesus and were called saints. Moreover, someone among them even committed the gross sin of having his father's wife; still Paul said they were sanctified in Christ Jesus. And furthermore, they were arrogant and self-important in their bearing, but Paul nonetheless acknowledged them as being sanctified in Christ Jesus. Thus we conclude that sanctification in the Bible does not refer to outside works. It is different from what Romans Chapters 5–8 say, for therein is presented the fruit of sanctification and not sanctification itself; because there it shows how each person should not be a slave to sin but should yield his members as instruments of righteousness so that he may produce the fruit of sanctification.

Our sanctification comes to us through the Lord Jesus Christ joining us to himself at His death. The tree is different from its fruit. The tree is a tree and fruit is fruit. Likewise, sanctification and the fruit of sanctification are different. Sanctification is one thing, its fruit is another. The believers at Corinth had their sanctified position, but they did not bear the fruit of sanctification. And it was for this reason that Paul wrote his letter to reprimand them, showing them how they must bear the fruit of sanctification as well as have their position of sanctification (2 Cor. 7.1).

"Of him are ye in Christ Jesus, who was made unto us wisdom from God, and righteousness and sanctification, and redemption" (1 Cor. 1.30). This verse reveals how Christ Jesus has become our righteousness, sanctification, and redemption. As Christ Jesus is righteous and holy before God, so we are righteous and holy in Christ. Our holiness before God is not any less than Christ's. Praise God, our holiness before Him is not based on our doing righteously. Holiness is not experiencing Christ, it *is* Christ. The holiness of Christ is our holiness.

"Such were some of you: but ye were washed, but ye were sanctified, but ye were justified in the name of the Lord Jesus Christ, and in the Spirit of our God" (1 Cor. 6.11). According to the order given here, it would seem that sanctification is ahead of justification. Paul says to his readers that they are already sanctified, they are already justified. Have we already been sanctified and justified? If you were to ask a Christian whether he is justified, he would boldly reply yes. You may even ask him if he is a righteous man and he would still dare to answer affirmatively. But suppose you ask him if he is a saint; most likely he will not dare admit himself to being a saint. Nevertheless, the Bible says we are already saints, we are already sanctified. Due to the Lord Jesus Christ, God not only forgives our sins and justifies us, He also reckons us as worthy, as being saints. This worthiness is that which is in the sight of God. Whenever we see ourselves, though, we are unable to enjoy this relationship.

"By which will we have been sanctified through the offering of the body of Jesus Christ once for all" (Heb. 10.10). Our sanctification is based on Jesus Christ offering up His own body. He does it once and it is accomplished forever: "By one offering he hath perfected for ever them that are sanctified" (v.14). Thank God, our sanctification is solely due to Christ, so ours is eternal and perfect. Some people are afraid to approach God because they always sense their uncleanness. Indeed, we *are* unclean and we can easily be defiled and turn unfaithful; nevertheless, we are holy because of Christ and not because of our own works. By the one offering of Christ we are sanctified forever. Our position before God is holy. Whenever we stand on that position and come to Him through Christ, He will look at us as being holy in Christ and will accept us as He has accepted Christ.

(c) *Bear the fruit of sanctification.* "Like as he who called you is holy, be ye yourselves also holy in all manner of living" (1 Peter 1.15). The Lord is holy, and we are called to a holy position; therefore, we must be holy in all manner of living. How ever can we claim to be holy before God and yet be unholy before men? We should show in our living that we are holy people, that we are set apart to God.

"Now being made free from sin and become servants to God, ye have your fruit unto sanctification, and the end eternal life" (Rom. 6.22). Praise God, having been made free from sin and sanctified to be servants of God, we should have the fruit of sanctification. We should not yield our members to lawlessness and unrighteousness; instead, we should yield our members to righteousness that we may belong wholly to God and bear the fruit of holiness as His servants.

"Having therefore these promises, beloved, let us cleanse ourselves from all defilement of flesh and spirit, perfecting holiness in the fear of God" (2 Cor. 7.1). We should rid ourselves of all the defilement of flesh and spirit—of all the things which are not of God—so as to bear the fruit of sanctification in the fear of God.

"Sanctify them in the truth: thy word is truth" (John 17.17). To be sanctified by truth is to bear the fruit of sanctification daily. For the truth is God's word. Daily we should examine our works with God's truth and rid ourselves of all that is dishonoring to God so that we may be cleansed. This is to be a progressive matter day by day, not something which it is assumed can be accomplished all at once. This is the work of the Holy Spirit who operates in us daily by the truth.

Some set forth the idea that sanctification is instantaneous and that we may be sanctified suddenly. Nothing of the sort. We may experience victory over sin suddenly, but we cannot call that sanctification. Sanctification is to be set apart to God; instant victory over sin is called deliverance. An erroneous interpretation will produce an erroneous effect.

"But he [the Father of spirits] [chastens us] for our profit, that we may be partakers of his holiness" (Heb. 12.10). Chastening is also a way for us to bear the fruit of sanctification. When our feet go astray we are turned back to God's way of holiness by His chastisement so that we may be partakers of His holiness and be entirely His.

Finally, let us see that the fruit of sanctification is not only a matter of our conduct but also a matter of our experience in nearness to and communion with God. "Follow after . . . sanctification without which no man shall see the Lord" (Heb. 12.14). No doubt we are sanctified positionally and we may boldly enter the holiest place so as to have intimate fellowship with God, but if we do not stand on the sanctified position with a true heart in fullness of faith, we seemingly will not be able to touch Him. Hence we must seek after holiness, since without it no man can see the Lord.

"And the God of peace himself sanctify you wholly; and may your spirit and soul and body be preserved entire, without blame at the coming of our Lord Jesus Christ. Faithful is he that calleth you, who will also do it" (1 Thess. 5.23,24).

TITLES YOU
WILL WANT TO HAVE

by Watchman Nee

Basic Lesson Series
Volume 1—A Living Sacrifice
Volume 2—The Good Confession
Volume 3—Assembling Together
Volume 4—Not I, But Christ
Volume 5—Do All to the Glory of God

Gospel Dialogue

God's Work

Ye Search the Scriptures

The Prayer Ministry of the Church

Christ the Sum of All Spiritual Things

Spiritual Knowledge

The Latent Power of the Soul

Spiritual Authority

The Ministry of God's Word

Spiritual Reality or Obsession

The Spiritual Man

The Release of the Spirit

by Stephen Kaung

The Splendor of His Ways

The Songs of Degrees
Meditations on Fifteen Psalms

ORDER FROM:
Christian Fellowship Publishers, Inc.
Box 1021
Manassas, Virginia 22110